cognitively unwell

Unstable Thoughts, Accurate Conclusions

By Lanie Ace

ISBN 978-1-972748-0-5

Library of Congress Control Number: 2026910078

Cover design and artwork by the author.

Published by,

Absent House Publishing, LLC
5025 Dell Range Blvd.
Cheyenne, Wyoming, USA
absenthousepublishing.com

This book is dedicated to a lot of people, so buckle up.

To everyone who has had to deal with me: the friends, partners, coworkers, teammates, strangers in grocery stores, and unfortunate souls who caught me mid–emotional spiral and thought, "Wow. This is…a lot." Thank you for staying. Or at least not calling animal control.

To the people who reached out after I said the quiet parts out loud. Who slid into my messages with, "Hey, I thought I was the only one," or "Reading that felt like someone cracked my rib cage and nodded knowingly." You trusted me with your stories, your shame, your late-night confessions, and your "me toos." This book exists because you reminded me that honesty echoes.

To my therapist for nodding calmly while I said absolutely unhinged things, for not calling the authorities when I described my coping strategies, and for repeatedly confirming that no, I am not in fact broken, just learning how to survive my trauma. Thank you for holding space while I fight my own brain like it owes me money.

To anyone struggling with mental health, the quietly drowning, the loudly unraveling, the high-functioning disasters, the exhausted survivors. If you've ever wondered whether you're too much, not enough, healing wrong, or failing at being a person, this is for you.

You're not weak.
You're not dramatic.
You're responding to things that mattered.

And finally, to my husband…my steady ground, my safe place, my emotional spotter. Thank you for loving me in all my forms: the feral, the frozen, the funny, the falling apart. Thank you for choosing me on the days I can't choose myself. You hold my hand while I learn how to stay alive in my own head, and that is not a small thing.

This book is for everyone who survived me, survived themselves, or is still trying.

I see you.
I love you.
And yes….you're allowed to laugh while you heal.

Contents

INTRODUCTION
A Love Letter to the Emotionally Feral

Alright, disaster gremlins, anxiety athletes, trauma scholars, and fellow creatures running exclusively on iced coffee and unresolved issues. You are about to enter the psychologically questionable universe of my mind.

A place where the floor is always emotionally lava, the coping skills are…let's call them "experimental," and the nervous system is permanently perched on a barstool whispering, "I swear to god, if one more thing happens today…"

Welcome to the book I absolutely did not intend to write, but apparently my brain had other plans.
(As usual. Does she ever ask permission? No. No she does not.)

This isn't a guide on how to become mentally healthy. If that's what you were hoping for, sweetheart, gently place this book down and run, don't walk, to someone who wears beige cardigans unironically and says things like, "Just do a gratitude list!" without blinking.

This book is for the rest of us.

The survivors.

The ones who healed wrong but kept going anyway.

The ones who wake up every morning and negotiate with their brain like it's a hostile raccoon inside a trash can.

The ones who don't trust compliments, don't know how to rest, and somehow still show up for life wearing emotional armor and a sarcastic smile.

This is for you if you've ever stared into the void and the void said, "Girl, same."

You are not broken. You are just…spicy.

Let me be very clear about something before we go further:

If you picked up this book because you feel like a malfunctioning human person, I'd like to formally welcome you to the club. We have jackets. They're all slightly too tight because trauma ruins posture, but we look incredible.

Here's the truth:

You are not broken.
You are not failing.

Your brain is doing its best with the absolute dumpster fire manual it was given.

Some of us were raised in emotional war zones and then judged for twitching when someone shuts a car door too loud.

Some of us weren't allowed to feel anything unless it was convenient for someone else.

Some of us were taught pride was unacceptable, joy was suspicious, and asking for help was morally equivalent to grand theft auto.

And then the world has the audacity to say:

"Relax!"
"Go with the flow!"
"Just be yourself!"

Be which self, Brenda? I have twelve. They rotate hourly.

This Book Is Not Here to Save You

I wish I could tell you this book will end with clarity.
With a breakthrough.
With a sentence that makes your brain shut the fuck up.

It doesn't.

This book will end the way most days do.
You're still inside your head.
Still carrying it.
Still navigating thoughts that feel heavier than they should.

No lessons neatly learned.
No villains defeated.
No "and then everything changed."

Living in your brain is hard.

Some days it's unbearable.
Some days it's just loud.

This book is not a cure.
I am not your savior.
There is no tidy redemption waiting at the end.

This is about naming the thing you've been surviving.
Because once you stop calling yourself broken for
surviving loudly, something shifts.

Not into peace, but into honesty.
And honesty, while not comforting, is at least real.

Your brain isn't broken.
It's just been through some shit.

Your Brain: A Choose-Your-Own-Adventure Book, but All the Options Are Traps

You're going to find chapters in this book about
suicidal ideation, self-harm, panic attacks, depression,
burnout, diagnoses with more letters than the alphabet,
and the raw emotional underbelly people don't talk
about unless it's 2 a.m. and everyone's trauma-bonding
in a kitchen.

But you're also going to find humor.

Because we have two choices when confronting the
darkness:

Cry.
Cry while laughing hysterically and making jokes that deeply concern our therapists.

We?
We choose the second one.

Your brain means well, I promise. It's like that overdramatic friend who's always doing the most:

"Oh, you got a compliment? PANIC."

"A relationship is going well? SELF-SABOTAGE."

"You felt joy for 0.3 seconds? SUSPICIOUS. ABORT."

It's not your fault.

It's your wiring.

Your nervous system is basically a smoke detector that goes off when someone makes toast.

And you're here reading this because deep down, under the panic, under the trauma goblin, under the depressive steamroller…you know you deserve something softer.

Something safer.

Something that doesn't require being emotionally flayed alive to "earn" love or peace.

This book isn't self-help. It's self-recognition.

Listen, I'm not here to fix you.

I can't.

I'm barely duct-taping my own consciousness together most days.

But what I can do is tell the truth.

The truth about the thoughts you've had but never admitted out loud.

The truth about the nights you've survived that nobody knows about.

The truth about the shame you've been carrying like a weighted blanket you didn't order.

I'm here to put language to things you've only ever felt as pressure in your chest.

I'm here to laugh with you at the absurdity of healing.

I'm here to tell you that the parts of you that feel unlovable are the exact parts that deserve the most tenderness.

You don't need fixing.
You need understanding.

You need permission to be human in a world that
rewards emotional robots.

You need someone to say,

"What you're feeling makes sense. You are not alone

 And also?

Same, babe. Same."

Part I:
The Brain That Won't Turn Off

Chapter 1
Welcome to the Brain That Will Not Let You Relax

Let's get this out of the way immediately:

If you are reading this book because you are fine, you are lost.

This is not a cozy little wellness journey where we sip lemon water and forgive our childhoods by page twelve.

There will be no gentle affirmations whispered over acoustic guitar.

No "have you tried mindfulness?" energy.

If that's what you're looking for, close the book and go hug a houseplant.

This book is for people whose brains wake them up at 3:17 a.m. like: "Hey. Remember everything you've ever done wrong? Cool. Let's review it in high definition."

This is for people who hear "just relax" and feel an immediate, irrational urge to commit light arson.

If your nervous system has ever mistaken a slightly loud noise for imminent death, welcome.

If happiness makes you suspicious, pull up a chair.

If you've ever thought,
"Wow, things are going well, can't wait for the

inevitable collapse,"
congratulations,
you're among peers.

If Your Brain Were a Building

If your brain were a physical location, it would be
condemned.

Yellow tape.
Structural damage.
A sign on the door that says:
"ENTER AT YOUR OWN RISK. MANAGEMENT IS
A LIAR."

Trauma does not give you a quiet inner voice.

It gives you a 24/7 group chat where everyone is
yelling,
nobody reads the room,
and at least one thought is absolutely convinced you're
about to ruin your entire life by breathing wrong.

There is no mute button.
There is no admin.
There is just chaos and a notification sound that feels
like a slap.

People love to say things like,
"Just listen to your thoughts."

No. Absolutely not.
My thoughts are unlicensed, uninsured, and actively
trying to start a fire.

My brain is not a calming sanctuary.

It is a haunted house run by raccoons with unresolved trauma and a megaphone.

The Morning Briefing

Every day starts the same way.
I wake up.
My eyes open.
And my brain immediately says something unhelpful, like:
"We forgot something important."
"Everyone secretly hates you."
"Today feels wrong. That's ominous."
"Remember that embarrassing thing from 2009? Let's relive it in IMAX."

Before I even get out of bed, my nervous system is already pacing like a bouncer outside a dive bar, cracking its knuckles, whispering, "I'm ready to overreact."

This is the part people don't understand about mental illness.
It's not always dramatic.
It's not always sobbing on the bathroom floor with mascara streaks and a sad playlist.

Sometimes it's just…constant.

A low-grade psychological static you can't turn off.

You can still go to work.
You can still answer texts.
You can still show up to dinner and laugh at the appropriate moments.

Meanwhile your brain narrating your life like it's trying to get you killed, fired, abandoned, or publicly humiliated…
sometimes all before noon.

And here's the betrayal:
The brain thinks its helping.

Your Brain Is a Safety System with Outdated Software

Somewhere along the way, probably during danger, neglect, abandonment, or chaos, your brain learned a rule:

"If I expect the worst, I won't be surprised when it happens."

So now it does that.
Relentlessly.
With no chill.

You get a compliment?
Your brain says, "They're lying. Don't fall for it."
You feel excited?
Your brain says, "Careful. This is how it starts."
Things are calm?
Your brain says, "Suspicious. Brace for impact."
Nothing bad is happening?
Your brain says, "Clearly you're missing something. Panic harder."

It's like living with an overprotective guard dog that bites *you* every time someone knocks on the door.

And the worst part isn't that the thoughts exist.
It's that they sound reasonable.
They don't show up wearing a villain cape.
They show up sounding logical.
Responsible.
Prepared.

They say things like:
"I'm just being realistic."
"I'm not negative, I'm prepared."
"Hope is costly."
"If we don't relax, we can't get hurt."

So you listen.
And slowly, quietly, your world gets smaller.
Your brain treats neutral moments like crime scenes.
It replays them from twelve angles.
Adds ominous background music.
Then convicts you of something vague but devastating.

This is not a flaw.
This is surveillance.
Your brain got loud because silence was never safe.

Silence is when things happened.
Silence is when nobody intervened.
Silence is when you learned to listen for danger like it
was a religion.

So now your thoughts sprint.
They overlap.
They interrupt each other.
They rehearse arguments that will never happen and
autopsy conversations that already died.
They bring up shit from ten years ago like its breaking
news.

Your nervous system has decided missing a detail is a capital offense.

The Floor Is Lava (Emotionally)

You cannot sit comfortably in good feelings.
Contentment feels itchy.
Peace feels like waiting for a jump scare.
Rest feels irresponsible.
Your brain whispers:
"Don't get used to this."
"This won't last."
"Enjoy it while you can."
"Who do you think you are being okay?"

So instead of standing in joy, you hover over it, knees bent, muscles clenched, jaw locked, like the floor is emotionally lava.

You don't experience good things.
You endure them.
And then you wonder why you're exhausted.

Living in your brain is exhausting not because you're doing too much, but because you're monitoring everything.

Tone shifts.
Facial expressions.
Silences.
Texts that end in periods instead of exclamation points.

Your brain is running background checks on reality like it's about to testify in court.

"Is that person mad at me?"

"Did I say something wrong?"
"Did I say too much?"
"Should I apologize?"

For what?
For existing?
Just in case?

Your body doesn't know you're safe.
It knows you're alive.
Those are not the same thing.

And people will say, "You're so high-functioning!"
Which is a deeply unhinged compliment.
Congratulations.
You can perform while internally combusting.
Gold star.

You're not dramatic.
You're conditioned.
Nobody is born flinching at happiness.
Nobody exits the womb thinking, "If I get too
comfortable, something bad will happen."

That's learned behavior.
That's survival training you didn't sign up for.

Your brain isn't pessimistic because it's broken.
It's pessimistic because optimism had consequences.

Hope made you visible.
Hope made you relax.
Hope made you assume.
And assumption was a luxury you couldn't afford.

So now your brain runs simulations instead.

"What if they're mad?"
"What if they leave?"
"What if I fucked this up?"
"What if I misunderstood?"
"What if I'm secretly unbearable and everyone is just being polite until they're not?"

The Brain That Won't Relax

This is the mind that keeps going.
The one that refuses silence.
The one that checks, rechecks, and checks again.
The one that keeps the lights on long after everyone else has gone home.

Not because it wants to.
Because it decided vigilance was the safest way to exist.
So it stays awake.
Watching.
Running simulations.
Waiting for problems that may never come.
And until something convinces it otherwise, it will continue doing exactly what it believes it was built to do:

Stay alert.

Chapter 2
Hypervigilance: Always On, Never at Peace

Hypervigilance is like living with a fire alarm that was installed directly into your spine and nobody ever gave you the shutoff code.

It never powers down.
It never takes weekends.
It does not respond to logic, reassurance, or the phrase "you're safe now."

Your body hears that and laughs like you just told it a cute joke.

Hypervigilance isn't anxiety's cousin.
It's anxiety's unhinged older sibling.
The one who grew up in chaos,
skipped therapy,
learned everything the hard way,
and now runs your nervous system like a private security firm with zero labor laws.

Your brain might think you're fine.
Your body is still on patrol.

Calm Is Not Calm. Calm Is Suspicious.

You don't relax.
You scan.

Who just shifted their tone?
Who stopped texting back?
Who's standing too close?
Who's being too quiet?

Where are the exits?
How fast can I leave if this goes sideways?

You don't sit in moments, you assess them.
You don't enjoy silence, you interrogate it.

Silence feels like the exact moment before something
bad happens.
So you stay ready.
Not because you're dramatic.
Because the last time you relaxed, something went
wrong, and your body remembers that part very clearly.

Prepared Is Not the Same as Afraid

Here's the thing people don't get:
Hypervigilance doesn't mean you're scared all the time.
That would be simpler.
It means your body is prepared all the time.

Prepared to fight.
Prepared to run.
Prepared to freeze.
Prepared to absorb impact like a human crumple zone.

Your nervous system never clocks out.
It doesn't rest.
It stands watch.

You are not anxious, you are on duty.

Why Everyone Thinks You're "So Put Together"

Most of the time, hypervigilance doesn't look like
panic.
It looks like competence.

You're observant.
You're "great with people."
You notice patterns others miss.
You anticipate problems before they happen.
You defuse tension without anyone realizing there was
a bomb in the room.

People praise you for it.
No one sees the cost.

They don't see your jaw permanently clenched like
you're bracing for a punch that never lands.
They don't see your shoulders living halfway up to
your ears.
They don't see that your breathing never quite reaches
the bottom of your lungs.
They don't see the exhaustion of being alert for decades
without relief.

Hypervigilance is socially rewarded until it breaks you.

Rest Feels like a Setup

Rest requires trust.
Trust that nothing bad is about to happen.
Trust that you don't need to be watching.
Trust that you won't regret letting your guard down.

Your body does not trust that.
Your body remembers what happened the last time you
relaxed.

So even on the couch.
Even in bed.
Even in objectively safe moments.
Some part of you is listening for footsteps.

For tone changes.
For threats only you seem to hear.

Your brain might be quiet.
Your body is not.

Joy Is Stressful When Visibility Is Unsafe

Hypervigilance ruins joy in a very specific way.
Joy makes you visible.
Visibility feels unsafe.

So even good moments come with tension:
Don't get too happy.
Don't get comfortable.
This is when it goes wrong.

You don't celebrate, you brace.
And then people ask why you seem distant, guarded, or
"unable to relax."

How do you explain that your baseline isn't "okay," its
"alert"?
That your nervous system has been in combat mode for
years with no ceasefire?

You Feel Responsible for Preventing Disaster

This is the quiet cruelty of hypervigilance:
You don't just feel unsafe.
You feel responsible.

If you miss a cue, your fault.
If you don't anticipate a mood shift, your fault.
If you relax too much and something goes wrong, your
fault.

Your nervous system believes vigilance equals survival, and anything less is negligence.

Hypervigilance turns existence into a full-time job with catastrophic consequences for mistakes.

And the most fucked-up part?
It works.

You do catch things others miss.
You do prevent problems.
You do keep things from exploding.

Which means your body gets reinforced every single time.

See?
Stay alert.
This matters.

The Danger Is Gone. Your Body Did Not Get the Memo.

People love to say, "You're safe now,"
like safety is a switch you forgot to flip.

Your body does not respond to reassurance.
It responds to patterns.
Consistency.
Time.
And even then, it might not believe it.

Because your nervous system learned safety the hard way, and it does not unlearn quickly.

Sometimes not at all.

Survival That Never Learned How to Stop

I'm not here to tell you to calm down.
I'm not going to tell you to do breathing exercises or
grounding techniques or "just relax."

Hypervigilance is what happens when survival works
too well.
It kept you alive once.
It does not know how to stand down.
So it watches.
It listens.
It anticipates.
It assumes that if you miss something, something bad
will happen, and it will be your fault.

You are not broken.
You are not dramatic.
You are not imagining danger where none exists.
You are living in a body that never learned what peace
feels like, and doesn't trust it when it shows up.

Always on.
Never at peace.
That's not a personality.
That's survival that never got the memo it was allowed
to stop.

Chapter 3
Anxiety: The World's Worst Bodyguard

Worry has sentences.
Anxiety has sirens.
Worry says, "What if?"
Anxiety says, "NOW."
No context.
No storyline.
Just your body slamming the panic button and snapping the fucking cover off so it can't be turned back off.

Anxiety doesn't protect you from danger.
It protects you from uncertainty.
And uncertainty is everywhere.

So your nervous system treats a lion, a neutral email, a missed call, and the produce aisle like they're all armed and actively hunting you.

"CODE RED."
"EVERYONE PANIC."
"PREPARE TO DIE."

Your Body Declares an Emergency without Asking Your Brain

This is the part that makes you feel insane.
There's no clear trigger.
No thought you can challenge.
No danger you can point at and say, "There. That's it."

Your heart spikes.
Your chest tightens.
Your hands sweat like you're defusing a bomb instead of picking avocados.

Your body has already decided something terrible is
happening.
You're just waiting to find out what.

And when your brain tries to catch up,
tries to logic its way in,
it's already too late.

Adrenaline has the wheel.
Cortisol's riding shotgun.
Reason is duct-taped in the trunk yelling, "Guys??"

Hypervigilance Is Exhaustion Disguised as Readiness

You don't relax.
You scan.

Rooms.
Faces.
Voices.
The tone of a text.
The pause before someone replies.
You sit facing exits.
You memorize escape routes from places you've been a
hundred times.
You rehearse conversations like they're hostage
negotiations.

You don't call it anxiety.
You call it being responsible.
But your body is guarding a VIP in an active war zone,
and the VIP is you.

Catastrophizing Is Pattern Recognition Gone Rogue

People love to call it irrational.
It's not.

Your brain isn't inventing fear out of nowhere.
It's extrapolating from experience.

Something went wrong before.
Shit followed.

So now your brain runs simulations nonstop.

Worst-case scenarios.
On loop.

Not to torture you.
To prepare you.
Preparation just feels like hell.

Anxiety learned early that calm was suspicious and
safety was temporary.
So now it treats everything like a potential ambush,
including joy.

A good day?
Extremely suspicious.

Bodily Panic Has No Plot

This is where CBT (Cognitive Behavioral Therapy)
advice goes to die.
There is no thought to challenge because the panic
didn't start in language.

It started in:
- Adrenaline.
- Cortisol.
- Muscle tension.
- Shallow breathing.

Your body reacts first.
Your brain shows up later, out of breath, holding a
clipboard like, "Okay but what if we just calm down?"
Too late.
You cannot reason with a guard dog mid-attack.

You Live Five Seconds From Impact

Even on good days.
Especially on good days.
You don't enjoy peace.
You brace during it.
Because peace has ended abruptly before,
and your body remembers.

So you live with your jaw clenched,
shoulders up,
breath shallow,
like you're trying not to be heard by a predator that may
or may not exist.

You are tired because your body thinks you are fighting
for your life.

All.
The.
Time.

Anxiety Makes Everything Feel Urgent

Your nervous system doesn't understand later.
Only now.
Everything feels equally critical.
Equally harmful.
Equally time-sensitive.

Emails feel like threats.
Decisions feel fatal.
Waiting feels unbearable.

And if you don't run?
Your body floods you with adrenaline anyway,
just to be safe.

People Think You're Overreacting Because They Can't Feel Your Body

They see the situation.
You feel the physiology.
They say:
"Relax."
"You're safe."
"It's not that serious."

Cool.
Now you're panicking and ashamed.
A two-for-one special.

Your heart races, your chest tightens, and then your
brain piles on with, "What the fuck is wrong with you?"

Helpful.

Anxiety Is Relentless, Not Loud

It's not always panic attacks.

Sometimes it looks like:
- Control.
- Over-planning.
- Avoidance.
- Irritability.
- Needing reassurance and hating yourself for needing it.

It's not dramatic.
It's constant.

Anxiety is the bodyguard who saved you once
and now won't stop kicking down doors,
tackling innocent bystanders,
and screaming about threats that exist entirely in her
own head.

She means well.
She just has the emotional regulation of a raccoon on
espresso.

You're Tired Because You're Always on Watch

You don't sleep deeply.
You don't rest fully.
You never stand down.
Your body stays armed even when nothing is
happening.

That level of vigilance costs energy.
No one sees the bill.

You Start Resenting Calm People

They say things like:
"I just trust it'll work out."
"I don't worry about that."

And you want to scream.

Because trust feels reckless when you've lived through consequences.

Your anxiety isn't pessimism.
It's memory.

This Isn't a Mindset Problem

Let's kill this lie.
You cannot positive-think your nervous system into safety.

This isn't about optimism.
It's about a body trained by experience to expect threat.

You're not failing anxiety management.
You're living inside a nervous system that learned danger early,
and learned it well.

No Coping List. Just Naming the Reality

I'm not going to tell you to breathe.
I'm not going to give you grounding exercises.
I'm not going to promise it passes quickly.

If you feel trapped inside your own alarm system.
If danger feels imminent without explanation.

If your body reacts faster than your thoughts.

That's anxiety.
Not worry.
Not weakness.

It's a hostage situation.

If you live like impact is always five seconds away…
If your body panics without permission…
If vigilance feels mandatory instead of optional…
You're not broken.
You're surviving inside a nervous system that learned
safety was conditional and threat was unpredictable.

And living like that,
day after day,
takes a kind of strength that never looks heroic
because it never gets a break.

Anxiety isn't fear of the future.
It's being trapped in a body that thinks the future is
already attacking.

And yeah,
she means well.
She just doesn't know when to stand the fuck down.

Chapter 4
Emotional Permanence Is a Scam

If I can't feel it, it doesn't exist.

Emotional permanence is the idea that feelings, connection, safety, and love continue to exist even when you can't actively feel them.

Which is hilarious.

Because the second something goes quiet, distant, delayed, or ambiguous, my brain assumes it has been revoked.

No text back?
Love is over.
Friendship is fake.
I am a burden who has finally been discovered.

Yesterday's reassurance?
Expired.
Nontransferable.
Void in all emotional states.

If I can't feel it right now,
it might as well be a myth.
Like unicorns.
Or stable mental health.

My Brain Has the Memory of a Goldfish with Trust Issues

People say things like,
"But you know they care about you."

No.

I knew they cared about me.

Past tense.

Feelings do not carry over in my system.
Affection has no shelf life.
Safety doesn't buffer.
Love doesn't persist off-screen.
Every interaction resets the board.

If you are not actively demonstrating care, my nervous system assumes abandonment has already occurred and I'm just late to the funeral.

Silence Is Not Neutral, It's a Verdict

Normal brains interpret silence as…silence.
Trauma brains interpret silence as:

- Punishment.
- Withdrawal.
- Proof you said too much.
- Confirmation you were tolerated, not wanted.

When someone goes quiet, my brain doesn't wait.
It convicts.
I replay everything I said.
Everything I didn't say.
Everything I shouldn't have said.

The conclusion is always the same:
I overdid it.

Again.

Reassurance Doesn't Stick. It Slides Right Off

People try.
They really do.

They reassure.
They explain.
They say, "Nothing changed."

But reassurance in my brain is like writing on a
whiteboard in the rain.

It's there.
Briefly.
Then gone.

I don't disbelieve people because I'm dramatic.
I disbelieve permanence because history taught me that
connection is temporary and safety has a curfew.

**Object Permanence but Make It Emotional and
Ruin My Life**

Babies cry when you leave the room because they don't
know you still exist.
Trauma does that to adults.

I intellectually understand you didn't disappear.
Emotionally?
You are gone until proven otherwise.

This is why:
- I panic when plans change.
- I spiral when routines break.
- I feel rejected by neutral behavior.
- I need reassurance I hate needing.

It's not clinginess.
It's a nervous system that learned connection could
vanish without warning.

"Just Remember the Good Times" Is a Joke

When I'm in it, I cannot access out of it.
When I feel unloved, I cannot remember being loved.
When I feel unsafe, I cannot remember safety.
When I feel alone, I cannot remember connection.

My brain does not time travel.
It traps me in whatever emotion is loudest.
So yes…
Yesterday I knew I was valued.
Today I am convinced I imagined it.

Both feel equally real.

This Makes Relationships Exhausting…for Everyone

Let's be honest.
This is not cute.
It's not quirky.
It's not endearing.
It's exhausting to love someone whose internal state
resets to "I am unlovable" every time the room goes
quiet.

It's exhausting for me, too.

I don't want to need reassurance.
I don't want to ask if we're okay.
I don't want to feel this fragile.
But emotional permanence didn't come installed.

It was removed by experience.

Trauma Taught Me That Good Things End Quietly

No explosions.
No closure.
No explanation.

Just distance.
Withdrawal.
Silence.

So now my body treats absence as danger.
It doesn't wait for evidence.

It remembers patterns.

And the pattern was:
Things leave.
People change.
You don't get warned.

Logic Knows Better. The Body Doesn't Care

You can explain emotional permanence to me all day.
You can say:
"They still love you."
"They're just busy."
"This doesn't mean anything."

My nervous system replies:
Show me.
Right now.
Or I will panic.

This isn't a thought problem.
It's a survival response.

I Don't Need Grand Gestures. I Need Continuity

I don't need intensity.
I don't need passion.
I don't need declarations.
I need consistency.

Because when connection flickers,
my system prepares for loss.
Not because I'm needy.
Because I've been trained by disappearance.

This Is Not About Fixing It

I'm not going to tell you how to build emotional
permanence.
I'm not going to offer tools.
I'm not going to suggest affirmations.
I'm not going to say "trust the process."

This is not a solution.
It's a confession.

If emotional permanence feels fake to you…
If reassurance evaporates the moment it's out of sight…
If silence feels like abandonment instead of space…
You're not broken.
You're not manipulative.
You're not trying to control people.
You're living in a nervous system that learned
connection was conditional and temporary.

Some of us don't forget love when it leaves the room.

We lose access to it.
And that doesn't make us weak.
It means something once disappeared when we needed
it most, and our body never forgot.

No answers.
No fixes.
Just the truth.
And honestly?
That truth explains a hell of a lot.

Chapter 5
When You're Too Self-Aware to Be Comfortable Anywhere

Congratulations,
you can see the matrix.
It sucks here.

Self-awareness is supposed to be a gift.
Insight.
Growth.
Emotional intelligence.
A gold star for knowing your patterns.

What they don't tell you is that once you see
everything,
you can't unsee it.

You don't just feel awkward in rooms anymore.
You understand why you're awkward,
how you're compensating,
which trauma response is driving the bus,
and how everyone else is also silently malfunctioning in
their own special way.

There is no bliss here.
Only analysis.

You're Never Just "In" the Moment

Other people are having experiences.

You are having:
- The experience.
- A running commentary.
- A diagnostic flowchart.
- A postmortem.
- A future regret simulation.

You notice their tone shift mid-sentence.
You clock the micro-expression you triggered.
You feel your nervous system activate before the conversation finishes.

You are inside yourself like it's a surveillance van.

Enjoy the party.

You Can Name the Problem but It Still Won't Shut Up

You know exactly what's happening.

This is hypervigilance.
This is a trauma response.
This is shame.
This is people-pleasing.
This is my abandonment wound tap-dancing.

Fantastic.

The knowledge does absolutely nothing to stop it.
Your body doesn't care that you've labeled the monster.

It still lives in the house

Every Interaction Feels like a Performance Review

You leave conversations exhausted,
not because they were bad,
but because you replayed them in 4K.

Did I talk too much?
Did I not talk enough?
Was that joke coping or avoidance?
Did I trauma-bond by accident again?
Did they feel obligated to listen?

You don't relax after socializing.
You audit.

And the auditor is mean.

You See Everyone's Damage and It Ruins Small Talk

Once you understand trauma, you can't unknow it.

You see:
- The insecurity behind confidence.
- The control under charm.
- The fear hiding in jokes.
- The loneliness dressed up as independence.

So when someone asks, "How are you?"
You have to choose between lying politely,
or detonating the conversation with the truth.

You usually pick lying.
Again.

You're Self-Aware Enough to Know You're Not "Normal"…But Too Aware to Pretend

You can't go back to ignorance.

You can't say:
"That's just how I am."
Because you know exactly how you became this way.

You can't say:
"I'm over it."
Because you know healing isn't a finish line.

You can't say:
"I'm fine."
Because you can hear the lie echo in your own skull.

So you exist in this limbo:
Too self-aware to bullshit yourself.
Too damaged to relax.
Too functional to be taken seriously.
Too honest to be comfortable.

Therapy Gave You Language but Stole Your Peace

Once you have words for everything, silence gets loud.
You notice when people project.
You notice power dynamics.
You notice emotional avoidance in real time.

You don't get to be naive anymore.
You know when someone is unsafe before they do.

Which means you're rarely surprised, and never at ease.

You Miss the Version of You That Didn't Know Better

This part feels illegal to admit.
Sometimes you miss when you didn't understand
yourself.

When you could react without commentary.
When you could feel without translating it into theory.
When you didn't know why everything hurt.

Self-awareness didn't cure your pain.
It just made it articulate.
Now your suffering has footnotes.

You Can't Turn It Off Without Dissociating

Relaxation feels suspicious.

If you're not analyzing, you're floating.
If you're not floating, you're scanning.
If you're scanning, you're tense.

There is no neutral gear.
So you oscillate between:
- Hyper-awareness
- Emotional distance

And people wonder why you seem "intense."

Buddy, this is me contained.

You're Not Wise. You're Tired.

People think self-awareness makes you enlightened.
What it actually makes you is exhausted.

You're carrying:
- Insight without relief.
- Understanding without resolution.
- Clarity without comfort.

You don't feel superior.
You feel overexposed.
Like you can see the cracks in everything,
including yourself,
and there's nowhere left to stand that feels solid.

Insight without Safety

Sometimes awareness is just the price you pay for
surviving long enough to understand what happened to
you.

If you're too self-aware to be comfortable anywhere…
If you can name every pattern but still can't rest…
If insight made you sharper but not safer…
You didn't fail therapy.
You didn't overthink yourself into misery.
You didn't ruin your own peace.
You adapted to a world where understanding was the
only thing that kept you from repeating the same pain.

You see clearly.
It hurts.
And you keep going anyway.

Which isn't growth porn.

It's not aspirational.

It's just what happens when awareness arrives before safety does.

Chapter 6
The "I'm Fine" Olympics

Welcome to the most exhausting competition you never signed up for.

There are no jerseys.
No medals.
No podiums.

Just a rigid spine,
a rehearsed smile,
and the unspoken rule that whoever breaks first loses.

You've been training for this longer than you realize.

The "I'm Fine Olympics" is a full-contact endurance sport where the goal is to appear functional while your internal organs are actively staging a coup.

You're not competing against other people.

You're competing against the fear of being labeled:
Needy.
Dramatic.
Too much.
Unstable.
Inconvenient.
Or the worst sin of all…honest.

"How are you?"
"I'm fine."
Translation: I am being held together by caffeine, dark humor, and the hope that I can fall apart later where no one can see me.

"Fine" isn't a feeling.
It's a ceasefire.

"Fine" Is a Strategic Lie, Not an Emotional State

You say it reflexively.
Automatically.
Before your brain even checks in with your body.

You say it at funerals.
You say it during panic attacks.
You say it while your chest feels like it's trying to
escape your ribcage like a feral animal.

"Fine" means:
- I don't want to explain.
- I don't trust what will happen if I do.
- I don't have the energy to manage your reaction.
- I am actively duct-taping myself together and
  calling it composure.

Somewhere along the way, you learned that truth came
with consequences.
That needing help made you a risk.
That emotional honesty made you a liability.
That struggling made you the problem.

So you adapted.
You didn't stop feeling things.
You just learned how to hide them better.

High-Functioning Is Just Collapse with Better Posture

Let's kill the most silencing compliment in mental
health:

"You're so strong."

No.
You're trained.

High-functioning doesn't mean healthy.
It means you learned how to bleed quietly.

You learned how to:
- Show up on time while hollow.
- Answer texts while dissociating.
- Support everyone else while ignoring your own body.
- Make jokes so no one asks follow-up questions.
- Apologize for taking up space while actively unraveling.

People praise this.
They call you resilient.
Put-together.
Impressive.

What they don't see is that you're running on emotional fumes and fear, powered entirely by the terror of disappointing literally anyone.

You didn't push through.
You dissociated through.

Dissociation: The Gold Medal Event

If there's a podium in the I'm Fine Olympics,
dissociation takes gold.
That moment when something should hurt, but doesn't.
When you slide just far enough out of your body to function without feeling.

You're present.
But not here.
You're responding.
But not connected.
You're smiling.
But it's muscle memory.

Dissociation isn't peace.
It's anesthesia.

It works.
Until it doesn't.

Until everything you postponed feeling shows up at
once like an overdue bill with compound interest.

But admitting that would require honesty.
And honesty feels exposing.

Why Admitting You're Not Okay Feels like a Threat

The second you say "I'm not okay," consequences enter
the chat.
People might worry.
People might ask questions.
People might expect things you don't have.
Or worse…people might dismiss it.

They'll say:
"You're fine."
"Everyone feels like that."
"But you seem okay."

Which is the emotional equivalent of being told your
house isn't on fire because the flames aren't visible
from the street.

So you keep competing.
You minimize your pain.
You compare your suffering to others.
You decide you haven't earned the right to complain.

You say "I'm tired" when you mean "I'm drowning."
You say "It's been a week" when you mean "I'm barely
holding it together."
You say "I'm fine" because it's the fastest way to end
the conversation.

When Someone Actually Notices (And Your Nervous System Panics)

And God help you if someone pushes.
If they look you in the eye and say,
"No. Really. How are you?"

Your nervous system reacts like you've been caught
committing a felony.

Too much truth feels threatening.
Too little feels fake.
So you offer a half-truth wrapped in a joke and hope
that's enough to escape without exposure.

This isn't pride.
It's survival.
You learned that vulnerability didn't lead to care, it led
to consequences.

So you became:
- Low-maintenance.
- Self-contained.
- Impressively functional while quietly falling
  apart.

The Quiet Escalation Nobody Sees

Here's the part people don't like to talk about.
When you suppress long enough, your brain starts
looking for exits.
Not always dramatic ones.
Not always permanent ones.

Sometimes it sounds like:
- "I just want everything to stop."
- "I don't want to die, I just don't want this."
- "I'm so tired of being in my own head."
- "How long am I supposed to keep doing this?"

That's not weakness.
That's your system waving a white flag.

Suicidal ideation doesn't always scream.
Sometimes it whispers.
Sometimes it offers relief.
Sometimes it just wants quiet.

And the cruel irony?
You worked so hard to seem okay that no one noticed
when you weren't.

"There Were No Signs" (Yeah. That Was the Problem.)

You became:
- The strong one.
- The reliable one.
- The one who handles things.

And one day you realized no one knew how bad it was,
because you never let them.

"There were no signs," they'll say.
Yeah.
That was the fucking problem.

No Medal. Just Exhaustion.

This isn't about opening up.
It's not about brave conversations or neat, inspirational
healing.
It's about naming the competition you were drafted into
without consent.

"I'm fine" wasn't honesty.
It was armor.
A strategy.
A lie you told so often it started to feel like truth.

There's no medal for that.
Just exhaustion.

And if "fine" is the best you can manage today?
Okay.
Just don't confuse surviving quietly with being okay
forever.
That's a different event entirely.

Chapter 7
Functioning Is Not the Same as Being Okay

Let's kill a very popular lie right now:
If you're functioning, you must be fine.

That's bullshit.

That's like saying a car running on fumes, duct tape, and spite is "doing great" because it hasn't exploded yet.

Functioning is the most convincing lie mental illness ever told.

Functioning looks great on paper.
Functioning gets praise.
Functioning keeps people off your back.
Functioning is showing up,
answering emails,
paying bills,
showering occasionally,
laughing at jokes,
and saying "I'm good" with enough confidence that no one asks follow-up questions.

Functioning is survival without a decent PR team.

Being okay, though?
Completely different sport.

Functioning Is a Performance, Not a Diagnosis

Functioning means:
- You showed up.

- You did the thing.
- You answered the email.
- You wore pants (optional, but impressive).

It does not mean:
- You're stable.
- You're healthy.
- You're coping.
- You're okay.

It just means you've learned how to move while bleeding internally.

Which, for the record, is not a flex.
It's a survival skill.

You can be functioning while your insides are held together with duct tape and resentment.
You can be functioning while fantasizing about disappearing, quitting everything, or sleeping for a year just to stop being on.

Functioning doesn't mean you're fine.
It means you're capable.

Capable of pushing through.
Capable of masking.
Capable of meeting expectations while quietly disintegrating.

And people fucking love that about you.

They say things like, "But you're doing so well!"
As if "well" is measured by output instead of internal damage.

You're not okay, you're operational.

High-Functioning Is Just Suffering With Better Lighting

"High-functioning" is the most gaslighting compliment ever invented.

What people mean is:
"Your pain doesn't inconvenience me."

You're articulate.
Capable.
Productive.
Funny about it.
So no one looks closer.

They don't see:
- The mental gymnastics required to get out of bed.
- The constant negotiation to stay alive.
- The emotional collapse scheduled for later, in private.

They just see output.
And they clap.

High-functioning mental illness is just pain with good manners.

You don't miss work.
You don't cancel plans.
You don't fall apart where anyone can see it.

You fall apart in the car.
In the shower.

At 2 a.m., staring at the ceiling, wondering how long you can keep this up.

You Learned Early That Falling Apart Wasn't an Option

You didn't become functional by accident.

You became functional because:
- No one was coming to save you.
- Needing help made things worse.
- Being "too much" had consequences.
- You had to keep going or everything would fall apart.

So you adapted.
You compartmentalized.
You minimized.
You swallowed everything and kept moving.
And now people expect that version of you forever.

Functioning becomes your identity.
Your proof of worth.
Your permission slip to exist.
Because as long as you're useful, you're allowed to stay.

Functioning Is How You Disappear in Plain Sight

Here's the deceptive part:
The better you are at functioning, the less likely anyone is to notice you're drowning.

You don't look like a crisis.
You don't sound like one.
You don't act like one.

So when you finally crack, people say,
"I had no idea."
You did.
You just didn't let yourself see it.

Because functioning convinces everyone,
including you,
that if you can still do things,
it can't be that bad.

Which is absolute bullshit.

You can function with a broken leg.
You can function with pneumonia.
You can function while bleeding internally.

Functioning is not evidence of wellness.
It's evidence of pressure.

You Don't Get Credit for the Effort It Takes

People don't see the internal cost.
They don't see the sheer force of will required to:
- Make decisions.
- Hold conversations.
- Regulate your tone.
- Not scream or vanish mid-day.

They see the result, not the labor.

So you start feeling crazy for how hard everything
feels.

Everyone else seems to be doing life on easy mode.
You're out here running it on expert difficulty with no
tutorial.

And then you use functioning against yourself.
"I went to work today, so I must be fine."
"I laughed, so it can't be that serious."
"I'm still getting things done, why am I complaining?"

Because you've confused endurance with health.

When You Finally Stop Functioning, Everyone Panics

Here's the fucked-up irony:
As long as you're functioning, no one worries.
The moment you can't?
Suddenly it's an emergency.
People scramble.
They ask what happened.
They act shocked.
As if your collapse came out of nowhere.
As if this wasn't the inevitable outcome of years of
carrying too much with no relief.

Stopping functioning is often the last thing to go.
Before that, you'll sacrifice:
- Sleep.
- Joy.
- Connection.
- Your body's signals.

Before you sacrifice productivity.

Functioning Becomes a Cage

At some point, functioning stops being empowering.
It becomes a trap.

You don't feel allowed to:
- Rest.
- Say no.
- Fall apart.
- Ask for help.

Because you've already proven you can handle it.
So now you should.
And every time you don't, you feel like you're failing
at the one thing you were good at.

Functioning keeps you alive, but it doesn't make life
livable.
It keeps the wheels turning while everything underneath
overheats.

You can keep going like that for a long time.
Longer than you should.
Longer than anyone realizes.
Longer than is fair.
Until functioning feels less like strength and more like a
hostage situation.

No Applause. Just Reality.

This is not a call to stop trying.
It's not a demand to implode publicly.
It's not a manifesto against responsibility.

It's just the truth people don't say out loud:
Functioning is not proof of wellness.
It's proof of endurance.
And endurance has a limit.

If you're functioning while miserable.
If you're keeping it together while falling apart inside.

If people tell you "you're doing great" and you want to
scream.
You're not ungrateful.
You're not dramatic.
You're not failing.
You're surviving in a world that rewards output and
ignores pain that doesn't disrupt the schedule.

There's no ending here where you magically become
okay.
No lesson about balance.
No neat resolution.

Just this:
You're allowed to be not okay even when you're still
getting shit done.

And if the only thing keeping you alive right now is
your ability to function…

That's not strength.
That's not weakness.
That's a person carrying more than they ever should
have had to.

Functioning can coexist with profound suffering,
and one does not cancel out the other.

And that truth deserves to be said out loud.

Chapter 8
Pride Feels like a Setup

Let's talk about the most suspicious emotion of all:
Pride.

Not shame.
Shame makes sense.
Shame is familiar.
Shame is the emotional equivalent of an old couch you
hate but know exactly where the springs are.

Not fear.
Fear is predictable.

Not sadness.
Sadness at least comes with snacks.

Pride?
Pride feels like bait.
Pride feels like the universe leaning in too close and
whispering, "Go ahead. Enjoy this. I dare you."

If you've ever accomplished something and your
immediate reaction wasn't joy but a low-grade sense of
impending doom, welcome.

Your nervous system has a long memory and absolutely
zero trust in good news.

For some of us, pride doesn't land as a celebration.
It lands as exposure.
Like standing naked under stadium lights while
someone in the distance sharpens a critique.

You finish something hard.
You survive something brutal.
You do something genuinely impressive.
And instead of "Holy shit, I did that,"
your brain says:
"Okay but who's about to notice?"
"Okay but when does this get taken away?"
"Okay but how exactly is this going to bite me in the
ass?"

Compliments don't feel kind.
They feel like reconnaissance.

Someone says, "You should be proud of yourself,"
and your stomach drops like ominous music just kicked
in.

Because pride makes you visible.
And visibility has never gone well.
Visibility meant scrutiny.
Visibility meant expectations.
Visibility meant someone deciding you were now fair
game.

So pride doesn't feel like confidence.
It feels like raising your head above the trench.

Your body reacts accordingly.

Heart racing.
Jaw clenched.
Shoulders tight like you're bracing for impact.

Joy activates your fight-or-flight response because joy
has historically been followed by punishment, loss,

humiliation, or the sudden realization that you jinxed
yourself by noticing something good.

So you downplay it.
You minimize.
You deflect.
You make a joke.

"Oh, it was nothing."
"I just got lucky."
"Yeah, but other people have done way more."

You shove your achievement under the rug like it's a
body and hope no one asks follow-up questions.

Because pride feels like tempting fate.

Visibility Has Historically Gone Bad for You

Here's the part nobody likes to say out loud:
You didn't learn this out of nowhere.

Somewhere along the way, you learned that happiness
made you a target.
That success invited commentary.
That confidence was mistaken for arrogance.
That joy was something people felt entitled to interrupt.

If you grew up in chaos, inconsistency, or conditional
love, good moments didn't last.

They were followed by:
A crash.
A punishment.
A withdrawal.
A reminder not to get comfortable.

So now joy feels less like relief and more like
foreshadowing.

If success used to invite scrutiny…
If praise came with strings…
If achievement was followed by "but you could've done
better..."
If happiness felt like tempting fate…
Then pride doesn't feel like celebration.

It feels like ringing a bell that says:
"Come humble me."

So when something goes right, your body doesn't relax.
It braces.

You don't feel proud.
You feel watched.

The Compliment Reflex: Duck and Cover

Something good happens and instead of celebrating,
your brain starts scanning.
"What's the catch?"
"What's coming next?"
"Who's going to ruin this?"
"How do I prepare?"

Someone says something nice about you and your brain
responds immediately:
"They don't mean it."
"They don't really know me."
"They're just being polite."
"This is going to age badly."

You don't settle into happiness.

You hover above it like it's a bomb you're trying not to
jostle.

You downplay.
You explain it away.
You apologize for it.

Not because you're humble.
Because accepting praise feels like signing a waiver for
future punishment.

Because somewhere deep in your body lives the belief:
"If I enjoy this too much, I will pay for it."

You learned that being seen too clearly made you a
target.
So now you shrink preemptively.
You neutralize joy before anyone else can.
You flatten yourself like it's a safety precaution.

When Good Things Trigger Panic

Here's a fun trauma trick nobody asked for:
You get good news.
Your chest tightens.
Your life gets calmer.
Your anxiety spikes.
You feel genuinely happy for half a second
and then your nervous system slams the brakes like:
"Abort. This is unsafe."

Because your body learned early that good things were
temporary.
That calm meant something bad was loading.
That joy came with consequences.

Pride doesn't feel empowering.
It feels reckless.

So instead of celebrating, you:
Downplay the win.
Obsess over what could've been better.
Prepare for disappointment.
Feel guilty for feeling good.

You don't celebrate.
You brace.

This isn't a confidence issue.
This is a threat response.

Your brain interprets pride as danger, physiologically.
Heart rate up.
Muscles tight.
Thoughts spiraling through every possible way this
could go wrong.

Your nervous system says:
"We are too visible. We are too relaxed. Something bad
is coming."

Happiness Feels like Lying

There's another layer people don't talk about:
Joy feels dishonest.
Because how dare you feel good when you're still
struggling.
When you still spiral.
When you still wake up some days tired of existing.

So happiness shows up and your brain says:
This isn't real.

This won't last.
I don't deserve this.

Instead of letting joy exist alongside pain,
you invalidate it entirely.
Because suffering feels more honest than happiness.

Pain feels earned.
Joy feels suspicious.

So you live in emotional middle ground.

Don't hope too hard.
Don't celebrate early.
Don't want things too much.
Because the less you want, the less can be taken.

You call it realism.
Your nervous system calls it safety.

"Who Do You Think You Are?"

There's usually a voice attached to this.
Sometimes it sounds like a parent.
Sometimes a teacher.
Sometimes a partner.
Sometimes a younger version of you who learned the
rules early.

It says:
"Don't get ahead of yourself."
"Stay small."
"Don't make a fuss."
"Pride comes before the fall."

So you keep yourself in check.

You avoid joy so it can't be ripped away.
You stay modest to the point of erasure.
You don't ask, "Why does this feel unsafe?"
You ask, "What's wrong with me?"

Nothing is wrong with you.
Something happened to you.

The Exhaustion of Never Letting Yourself Win

Do you know how tiring it is to never let anything land?
To never rest in success?
To constantly wait for the other shoe to drop?

It's emotional hypervigilance dressed up as humility.

You don't feel proud.
You feel relieved.
And even that relief is brief.
Because your system doesn't know how to hold good
things without flinching.

This isn't arrogance.
This isn't ego.
This isn't a self-esteem problem.
This is about safety.

Your body does not feel safe being seen.
It does not feel safe being praised.
It does not feel safe being happy without consequences.

You cannot mindset your way out of a nervous system
that learned survival the hard way.

Here's the truth without the inspirational ending:
You didn't reject pride because you don't deserve it.

You rejected it because it never felt safe to keep.

And maybe the hardest part isn't learning how to feel proud.
It's admitting that part of you is still waiting to be punished for doing well.

If pride feels like a setup, it's because once upon a time, it was.

And you're allowed to be complicated about that.

Chapter 9
Burnout Isn't a Phase, It's a Personality Trait

Burnout isn't something you enter.

It's something you realize you've been living in when someone asks how you are and you have to scroll through several internal error messages before answering.

Burnout doesn't feel like a bad week.
It doesn't feel like a mood.
It doesn't feel like something a long weekend and a candle named Forest Escape can fix.

That idea is adorable.

Burnout is not being tired.
Burnout is exhaustion that got comfortable.

It's exhaustion that unpacked its bags, changed the furniture, and started introducing itself as your personality.

It's waking up tired.
Staying tired.
Going to bed tired.
And somehow still feeling guilty for it, like rest is a character flaw and sleep is something you haven't earned yet.

You don't remember what "rested" feels like anymore.

You just remember different flavors of tired.
Functional tired.
Crying-in-the-shower tired.

Staring-at-the-wall-like-a-haunted-doll tired.
I could sleep twelve hours and still wake up resentful
tired.

Burnout didn't happen overnight.
It crept in quietly, wearing productivity as a disguise.

At first it looked like ambition.
Then responsibility.
Then survival.

Somewhere along the way, exhaustion stopped being a
warning sign and started being your default setting.

And instead of asking why, you adjusted your
expectations downward and called it maturity.

You don't say "I'm burned out."
You say, "This is just how I am."
You don't say "I need a break."
You say, "I'll rest after this one last thing."

Which is funny, because there is always one last thing.

When Exhaustion Becomes Identity

At some point, being tired stopped being a state and
became a character trait.

You don't say "I'm exhausted."
You say, "Yeah, that tracks."

Exhaustion implies rest would help.
Burnout laughs at rest.

You can sleep for ten hours and wake up feeling like
you ran a marathon in wet cement while being yelled at
by your own thoughts.

Your bones are tired.
Your brain is tired.
Your will is tired.

Not "I need a nap" tired.
"I have no internal resources left" tired.

You're not sad in a dramatic way.
You're not anxious in a productive way.
You're not even angry in a clean, motivating way.

You're empty.

And irritated that people expect you to bounce back like
nothing happened.

You didn't lose your spark.
It was consumed.

You don't remember the last time you felt rested, but
you remember years of pushing through because:

Someone needed you.
Something depended on you.
Stopping felt disallowed.
Collapse was not an option.

So you adapted.
Of course you did.

You learned how to function on fumes.
How to show up hollow.

How to keep going long after your body started quietly begging you to stop.

Now you're shocked that everything feels heavy, joyless, and vaguely unbearable.

Rest Feels like a Threat, Not a Reward

Here's the fucked-up part no one warns you about:
When you're burned out, rest doesn't feel good.
It feels wrong.

Rest feels like:
  * Falling behind.
  * Being judged.
  * Being lazy.
  * Being replaceable.
  * Being punished.

The moment things slow down, your brain goes,
"Cool. Now we can finally panic."

You sit still while mentally sprinting.
You take time off and feel guilty the entire time.
You try to recharge and end up more exhausted because your body never learned how to be off-duty.

Silence gets loud.
Stillness brings memories.
Stopping means feeling.
And feeling is exactly what your system has been avoiding to survive.

So you stay busy on purpose.

You overcommit.
You doom-scroll.
You say yes when you mean no.
You exhaust yourself intentionally because being tired
is safer than being present.

Burnout isn't accidental.
It's protective.

Exhaustion keeps you moving.
Exhaustion keeps you numb.
Exhaustion proves you're trying.

You wear it like a badge of honor and a threat at the
same time.

Look how much I can handle.
Look how much I endure.
Look how close to the edge I live and keep going
anyway.

Productivity Is a Trauma Response, Actually

Let's call this what it is.

Some of you aren't driven.
You're afraid.

Afraid that if you stop:
- You'll fall apart.
- You'll feel how bad it actually is.
- You'll be useless.
- You'll disappoint everyone.

So you keep moving.
You stay productive.

You tie your worth to output like your life depends on
it.

Because once upon a time?
It did.

You were praised for achieving.
You were valued for performing.
You were noticed when you were useful.

So now doing nothing feels like social death.

Burnout isn't laziness.
It's the cost of earning your right to exist.

Productivity Culture Can Eat My Entire Ass!

We live in a world that rewards burnout and calls it
ambition.

Push harder.
Do more.
Be grateful you're busy.
Hustle until you collapse,
then blame yourself for collapsing wrong.

Burnout gets treated like a personal failure instead of
the predictable outcome of living too long without
safety, support, or relief.

Spoiler: you are not a machine.
You are meat with feelings and a nervous system that
keeps receipts.

Burnout Doesn't Just Make You Tired

It makes you angry.

Angry at stupid things.
Angry at small things.
Angry at people breathing too loud.

You snap.
You withdraw.
You resent and then feel guilty for resenting.

You don't want to be needed.
You don't want to be asked for anything.
You don't want to be touched.
You don't want to explain yourself.
You want to disappear, but not die.

Just be unreachable.

That doesn't make you cruel.
It makes you depleted.

Burnout is grief wearing work clothes.

Grief for the version of you who had energy.
Grief for the dreams that now feel exhausting.
Grief for the life you thought you'd have if you could
just get through one more thing.

Spoiler:
There was always another thing.

The Collapse Nobody Warned You About

People expect burnout to look dramatic.
Tears.
Breakdowns.
Quitting everything and moving to the woods.

Sometimes it does.
But more often?
It looks like numb efficiency.

You still get things done.
You just don't care.
You cross things off lists without feeling anything.
You accomplish things that used to excite you
and feel nothing but relief that it's over.

You're not energized by success.
You're just glad it's finished.

That scares people.

Because apathy doesn't beg for help.
It just quietly erodes your life.

Unchecked burnout escalates.
You stop caring.
You stop feeling.
You start fantasizing about quitting everything with
zero plan.

You think:
"I can't do this forever."
"I don't have anything left."
"If this is life, I'm not interested."

That's not drama.
That's capacity.

This Is the Part with No Redemption

Here's the truth without the inspirational ending:
Your body will stop you eventually.
The only question is how violent it has to be to get your
attention.

Burnout doesn't mean you failed.
It means you survived longer than you should have had
to.

You didn't choose burnout.
You adapted into it.
And now it's stitched so deeply into your identity that
imagining a life without exhaustion feels more
uncomfortable than continuing to live inside it.

Not because you like it.
But because it's all you've ever known.

There's no miracle reset here.
No glowing comeback story.
No "and then everything changes."

Sometimes burnout doesn't resolve.
Sometimes it just becomes the background condition
you learn to live inside.

You mourn your old capacity.
You stop pretending you can do what you used to.
You adjust your life around the damage.
And that grief doesn't get enough credit.

If you're burned out, you're not broken.
You're overextended.

If everything feels like too much, it's because it is.

There's no badge for surviving burnout quietly.

You're still here in a body that finally said enough.

And even if you never get your old energy back,
that doesn't mean you failed.

It means the cost was real.

Chapter 10
Imposter Syndrome: Everyone's going to Find Out
I'm a Fraud

Let's be honest.
Imposter syndrome is not a cute little confidence
wobble.

It's a chronic condition where your brain insists you
accidentally broke into your own life and security is
about to escort you out.

Any minute now.

You're not successful, you're undetected.
You're not competent, you're lucky.
You're not talented, you're temporarily convincing.

And the better you do, the worse it gets.
Because imposter syndrome doesn't say,
"You're bad at this."
It says, "You're about to be caught."

You don't feel accomplished.
You feel exposed.

Every win feels temporary.
Every compliment feels misdirected.
Every success feels like evidence the audit is coming.

You're not proud, you're alert.

Success Feels like Exposure, Not Proof

Here's the trick imposter syndrome pulls every time:
Achievement doesn't feel like belonging.

It feels like a spotlight.

You don't think, "I did that."
You think, "Oh fuck. Now they're looking at me."

Praise lands like bait.
Recognition feels like surveillance.
You're waiting for the follow-up email.
The meeting.
The pause where someone finally says,
"So…can you explain how you did that?"

And you'll freeze.
Stumble.

Reveal the truth…that you're not actually competent,
just traumatized enough to over-perform convincingly.

Because somewhere along the way,
your nervous system learned that visibility meant
judgment,
correction,
humiliation,
or being taken down a peg for sport.

So even when you're winning, you shrink.

You Don't Trust Praise Because You Were Trained Not To

When someone says you did a good job, your brain
immediately starts cross-examining the moment.

"Are they being polite?"
"Do they want something?"
"Are they just wrong?"

You don't absorb praise.
You deflect it like it's radioactive.

"Oh, it was nothing."
"I just got lucky."
"Anyone could've done this."

Anyone didn't.
You did.

But claiming that feels costly.
Because pride feels like tempting fate,
and fate has historically been a dick.

You live in the gap between how you look and how you
feel.

From the outside, you seem capable.
Put together.
Legitimate.

Inside, you feel like you're winging it on vibes,
caffeine, and a rapidly degrading nervous system.

So you over-prepare.
Over-deliver.
Over-explain.

You build a fortress of competence so thick no one can
see how terrified you are underneath it.

And it works.

People call you smart.
Capable.
Impressive.

You nod politely while internally screaming,
"You are all making a huge mistake."

Imposter Syndrome Is Not Insecurity. It's Prosecution.

This isn't self-doubt.
This is your own mind acting like internal affairs.

It's not asking, "Am I good enough?"
It's building a case for why you don't belong.

You re-read emails.
You obsess over tone.
You rehearse explanations for mistakes that haven't
happened yet.

You don't ask for help,
not because you don't need it,
but because questions feel incriminating.

You don't say "I don't know,"
because that feels like handing over evidence.

So you stay hypervigilant.
Forever auditioning for a role you already have.

Trauma Loves Imposter Syndrome

If you grew up having to prove your worth,
earn your place,
justify your existence,
stay useful to stay loved,
then belonging never felt guaranteed.
It felt conditional.
Temporary.

Revocable.

So even when you earn it, you don't trust it.

Your nervous system learned:
- Love is conditional.
- Approval is temporary.
- Safety depends on performance.
- Mistakes are costly.

So success doesn't calm you.
It raises the stakes.
Because now there's more to lose.

Failure Feels Inevitable

There's a quiet belief humming under all of this:
"This will end."
You don't know how.
You don't know when.
You're just sure it's coming.

So you don't enjoy success.
You manage it.
You plan for the fall.
You rehearse apologies.
You soften expectations before someone else can.

You compare yourself to everyone and always lose.
Everyone else seems more confident.
More deserving.
More legitimate.
Less exhausted by existing.
You ignore context.
You ignore different paths.

You ignore the fact that you can't hear their internal
monologue screaming at 3 a.m.

You only hear yours.
And you treat it like evidence.

Liking What You Do Makes It Worse

And God help you if you actually like what you're
doing.
Liking it makes you invested.
Liking it makes you visible.
Liking it means it will hurt more when you're
inevitably exposed.

So you keep one foot emotionally out the door.
You stay ready to leave before you're pushed.
You tell yourself it was never that serious anyway.

This is how you survive imposter syndrome:
By never fully arriving.

You achieve things while hovering above them.
You accept praise like it's a misunderstanding you're
too polite to correct.
You downplay your role because owning it feels like
inviting disaster.
Because if you claim your competence and then fail, it
won't just be a mistake.
It'll be proof.

No Confidence. No Resolution.

This isn't about suddenly believing in yourself.
Sometimes imposter syndrome softens.
Sometimes it doesn't.

Sometimes it just follows you into bigger rooms
wearing a nicer outfit.
That doesn't mean you're secretly unqualified.
It means your nervous system learned early that
belonging was fragile.

Here's the raw truth:
You're not afraid you're bad.
You're afraid you're temporary.
And until that fear loosens its grip, every success will
feel less like a victory and more like borrowed time.

No cure.
No pep talk.
No "you earned this" bow tied on the end.

Just the reality of doing the thing anyway, while your
brain whispers you don't belong.

And the deeply uncomfortable knowledge that you're
allowed to keep going, even if you never fully believe
it.

Part II:
When The Lights Go Out

Chapter 11
Depression Isn't Sadness. It's Static. (And It Eats Motivation for Sport)

If anxiety is a body screaming RUN, depression is a brain quietly unplugging the speakers and saying, "Why bother?"

If depression were just sadness, everyone would understand it.

Sadness cries.
Sadness is loud.
Sadness at least has the decency to feel like something.

Depression is static.
It's the low-level hiss under everything.
Emotional white noise that never shuts the fuck up,
but also never says anything useful.
Just constant interference that makes every thought fuzzy,
every feeling muted,
every action feel like it requires a permission slip you never received.

Depression doesn't scream.
It erodes.

It doesn't say, "I'm miserable."
It says, "What's the point?"

And it says it casually.
Like it's just stating a fact everyone else already accepted.

Depression isn't crying on the bathroom floor with
dramatic music swelling in the background.
Depression is staring at the wall for forty minutes
because starting anything feels like trying to lift a
refrigerator with your eyelashes.

Sadness has texture.
Depression has absence.

It's not that everything hurts.
It's that nothing registers.

The Lie That Depression Is Just Being "Down"

People love to say things like:
"Everyone gets depressed sometimes."
"You just need to think positive."
"Try going outside."

Yes.
Everyone feels sad sometimes.
Depression is not that.

Depression is waking up and realizing the day already
defeated you and it's only 8:14 a.m.
It's food tasting like cardboard.
Music sounding flat.
Texts feeling impossible.
Showering requiring negotiations.
Joy feeling theoretical.

You're not sobbing.
You're not dramatic.
You're just…offline.

When Everything Feels Heavy for No Reason

Here's the cruelest part:
Depression doesn't need a cause.
You can have a job.
People who care about you.
No immediate crisis.
A life that technically looks fine.
And still feel like you're wading through wet cement
just to exist.

That's where the shame creeps in.
You start thinking:
I have no right to feel like this.
Other people have it worse.
What the fuck is wrong with me?

Nothing is wrong with you.
Your brain chemistry is being a dick.

Depression Makes You Bad at Existing

Depression turns basic life tasks into moral failures
inside your own head.
You don't reply to messages → You're a terrible friend.
You cancel plans → You're flaky and unreliable.
You can't clean → You're lazy.
You can't focus → You're stupid now.

Depression doesn't just drain energy.
It narrates the experience like a hostile documentary.
And the worst part?
It sounds convincing.

The Numb Phase (Which Is Somehow Worse)

Here's the part people don't expect:
Depression doesn't always hurt.
Sometimes it just hollows.

You don't feel devastated.
You don't feel dramatic.
You don't feel anything strongly enough to justify
concern.

You wake up and the world looks the same, but flatter.
Muted.
Like someone turned the saturation all the way down
and forgot to turn it back.

Music doesn't hit.
Food tastes like texture.
Things you used to love feel…neutral.

And that's worse than sadness.
Because sadness proves you're still connected to
something.

Depression is disconnection.
People will say, "Isn't numb better than upset?"
No.
It's terrifying.
Because when nothing matters,
everything becomes optional.
And that's when depression gets precarious.

Not loud.
Not dramatic.
Just quiet and persuasive.

When the Thoughts Turn Dark (Without Warning)

Depression doesn't usually say, "I want to die."
More often it says:
"I don't care if I wake up."
"I'm tired of being here."
"This is pointless."
"Everyone would adjust."

These thoughts don't arrive with sirens.
They drift in like background noise.
And people feel immense shame for them,
because they didn't ask for them,
but now they're there.

Depression doesn't want you dead.
It wants you indifferent.
It wants you to stop reaching.
Stop hoping.
Stop investing energy in things that might disappoint
you.

Thoughts are not intentions.
Thoughts are symptoms.
Having them doesn't make you unstable.
Pretending they aren't happening does.

Depression Eats Motivation like It's a Competitive Sport

Depression doesn't just lower motivation.
It devours it.
Olympic-level consumption.
No crumbs left behind.

You don't feel lazy.
You feel glued to the floor by gravity you can't see.
Everything feels heavier than it should.
Including your own body.

Getting started is impossible.
Finishing doesn't feel good either.
There's no satisfaction.
No reward.
Just relief that it's over.

You don't think, "I did it."
You think, "Thank god that's done."

Joy doesn't register.
Accomplishments don't land.
Compliments bounce off like rubber bullets.
People tell you to "find your passion again,"
as if depression didn't already pawn that shit for
cigarettes and rent money.

Passion isn't missing.
It's inaccessible.

Buried under apathy, exhaustion, and a constant
internal shrug that says, "Cool. Still don't care."

Depression Is Exhaustion without Relief

Sleep doesn't fix it.
Rest doesn't reset it.
Weekends don't cure it.

You're tired in a way that feels cellular.
Your bones are tired.
Your thoughts are tired.

Your soul,
if you believe in that sort of thing,
is slumped in a chair asking when this ends.

Sometimes things help.
Sometimes they don't.
Sometimes you do everything "right" and still feel
empty.

And that's where people get uncomfortable.
Because effort without results threatens the idea that
mental health is a neat equation you can solve if you try
hard enough.

Depression doesn't care about your plans.
It doesn't care about your progress.
It just exists.

It robs you of anticipation.
Nothing feels worth looking forward to,
not because nothing is good,
but because your brain can't access the feeling of
wanting.

You Are Not Lazy. You Are Depressed.

Say it again.
You.
Are.
Not.
Lazy.

Depression is not a motivation problem.
It's a capacity problem.
It's waking up with your internal battery already dead.
There is no reserve energy.

There is no hidden potential waiting to be unlocked.
You're not unmotivated.
You're depleted.
And the more you shame yourself for it, the heavier it
gets.

The Isolation Spiral

Depression isolates you,
then convinces you that you deserve to be isolated.
You pull away because interacting is exhausting.
Then you feel guilty for pulling away.
Then you pull away more.

It tells you:
"You're a burden."
"No one wants to hear this."
"You're ruining the vibe."

So you go quiet.
Quiet feels safer.
Until it doesn't.

Depression Is a Liar with a Calm Voice

Anxiety screams.
Depression whispers.

It tells you:
"This is just who you are now. You don't actually like
anything."
"This is adulthood. Trying won't change anything."

And because it's quiet, you believe it.

Numbness feels factual.
Hopelessness feels logical.
Depression is excellent at erasing your memory of
anything that contradicts it.

Not a Crisis, Just Stuck

This isn't rock bottom.
This is the plateau.
The endless, colorless middle where nothing is wrong
enough to demand attention and nothing is right enough
to feel worth pursuing.

And that's what makes it insidious.
Because it doesn't look like crisis.
It looks like a personality.
You start thinking, "Maybe this is just who I am now."

Low-energy.
Disengaged.
Permanently unimpressed by life.

There's no dramatic ending here.
No triumphant reclaiming of joy.
No swelling music when the static clears.

Depression doesn't break you loudly.
It wears you down quietly.

Surviving it doesn't look brave or inspirational.

It looks like continuing to exist in a world that feels
muted,
heavy,
and deeply unmotivating,

while everyone assumes you're fine because you're still standing.

Which, somehow, you are.

And that's not poetic.
It's not hopeful.
It's just real.

And sometimes, that's all there is.

Chapter 12
Self-Loathing: My Brain's Favorite Hobby

Self-loathing isn't an occasional thought.
It's a subscription service my brain signed me up for
without consent.
Auto-renew enabled.
No cancel button.
Customer service permanently closed.

If self-loathing burned calories,
I'd be shredded.

Not in a hot way.
In a clinically concerning way.

It runs in the background while I brush my teeth,
while I drive to work,
and while I exist near other humans.

It critiques my tone,
my face,
my posture,
my personality,
my past,
my future,
and my general right to take up oxygen.

It never takes a day off.

And the most fucked-up part?
It sounds like me.
That's how it gets away with it.

The Voice Didn't Start With You

Here's the first lie self-loathing tells:
"This is just how I am."
Nope.
That voice is inherited.

It's a Frankenstein mashup of:
- Adults who criticized instead of protected.
- Authority figures who confused control with care.
- Systems that rewarded perfection and punished need.
- A world that taught you love was conditional and failure was punishable.

You didn't wake up one day and decide to hate yourself.
You were trained.

Self-loathing didn't drop out of the sky.
It was installed slowly,
quietly,
through repetition.
Through being corrected more than comforted.
Through learning that being hard on yourself kept you sharp,
compliant,
acceptable.

So you internalized the criticism before anyone else could say it.
You beat them to the punch.
If you say it first, it hurts less.
If you hate yourself preemptively, no one else gets the satisfaction.

Internalized Cruelty Wears a Sensible Outfit

Self-loathing doesn't show up screaming, "You're worthless."
That would be too obvious.
It shows up dressed as responsibility.
"I'm just being honest with myself."
"I need to be accountable."
"I can't let myself get lazy."
"Someone has to keep me in check."

That's not discipline.
That's abuse with a productivity planner.

If someone talked to you the way your brain does,
you'd tell them to get fucked and file a restraining order.
But because it's your voice now, it gets a pass.

Self-loathing wears the voice of reason and calls it honesty.

You Hate Yourself for the Symptoms of What Hurt You

This is the cruelest loop:
You struggle because you were hurt.
Then you hate yourself for struggling.

You judge your anxiety.
You despise your depression.
You shame your burnout.
You attack your trauma responses.

As if these things appeared out of nowhere just to inconvenience you.

As if your nervous system is a moral failure.
As if surviving left you no right to be tired.

It tells you you're lazy when you're exhausted.
Dramatic when you're overwhelmed.
Broken when you're reacting exactly how a nervous
system reacts after too much shit.

And it never shuts up.

You can do ten things right and it will autopsy the one
thing you did weird.
You can receive genuine praise and it will immediately
discredit the source.
"They don't really know you."
"They're just being polite."
"If they saw the real you, they'd change their mind."

Self-loathing does not accept evidence.
It rewrites it.

Self-Loathing Is Control When Everything Else Feels Out of Control

Self-loathing feels productive.
If you're already punishing yourself,
no one else can do worse.
If you stay ahead of the criticism, you won't be
blindsided.
If you hate yourself first, rejection hurts less.
So your brain keeps the insults coming like it's doing
you a favor.

It's not trying to destroy you.
It's trying to manage risk.
It's just terrible at it.

Self-loathing becomes armor.
Heavy, rusted armor that cuts you every time you move,
but hey,
at least you're protected.

The Greatest Hits Playlist (You Know All the Words)

Let's run the classics:
- "Everyone else manages this. Why can't you?"
- "You're exhausting."
- "You're too much."
- "You're broken."
- "If you were stronger, this wouldn't be happening."
- "You're embarrassing."
- "You should be better by now."

Notice how none of these actually help.

They don't motivate.
They don't solve.
They don't protect.
They just keep you small and tired.
Mission accomplished.

You Learned to Confuse Worth with Performance

Somewhere early on, worth got tied to output.
How useful you were.
How easy you were.
How impressive you were.
How quiet you were about needing anything.
So now, on days you can't perform?
You don't feel neutral.

You feel worthless.
Not struggling...defective.

And instead of compassion, your brain reaches for
contempt.
Because contempt is familiar.
Especially when you're functional.

Self-loathing thrives on performance.

As long as you're doing well externally, it convinces
you that the only reason you haven't failed completely
is because you're being hard enough on yourself.

"See? This works. Don't stop."

So you don't.
You drive yourself with shame.
You motivate yourself with fear.
You keep yourself in line with cruelty.
And people call you disciplined.

They don't hear the internal abuse.
They don't hear the constant barrage of "not good
enough, not yet, not like this."

Self-Loathing Doesn't Want You Dead

This matters.
Self-loathing doesn't want you dead.
It wants you small.
Second-guessing.
Apologizing.
Shrinking your needs until they're barely detectable.

It wants you so busy managing your flaws that you
never question why you're the only one being punished.

And when someone says, "Be kinder to yourself,"
your brain laughs like that's a cute suggestion.

Kindness feels unsafe.
Softness feels irresponsible.
Self-compassion feels like letting a criminal off without
consequences.
Because if you stop hating yourself, who's going to
keep you in check?

That's the lie.

You Don't Need Encouragement, You Need the Knife Put Down

People think the antidote to self-loathing is
affirmations.
It's not.

Telling someone who hates themselves to "be nicer" is
like telling someone who's drowning to "just float."

Self-loathing isn't a lack of positivity.
It's an excess of violence turned inward.
Your brain learned that criticism kept you safe,
compliant, and acceptable.
So it sharpened that tool.
And now it won't let go.

I'm not going to tell you to love yourself.
I'm not going to tell you to reframe.
I'm not going to tell you to be grateful for your
resilience.

That shit doesn't land when you're deep in it.

Sometimes the most honest goal isn't self-love.
It's ceasefire.

Not hating yourself for five minutes.
Not attacking yourself for struggling.
Not adding more pain to pain.
That's not healing.
That's harm reduction.

Self-loathing isn't honesty.
It's repetition.
It's trauma echoing in your own voice.
And surviving with it doesn't make you weak or
pathetic or broken.

It means you've been living with an internal narrator
who hates you and refuses to shut the fuck up.
Which is not a personal failure.
It's just another thing you learned in order to survive.

Self-loathing is not insight.
It's not discipline.
It's not honesty.
It's a survival strategy that outlived its usefulness.
And you're allowed to be fucking exhausted by it.

Chapter 13
Rest Feels Dangerous and I Don't Know How to Stop

"Just rest" is the most violent advice I've ever heard.

People say "just rest" like it's a button.
Like you flip a switch,
lie down,
exhale,
and your nervous system doesn't immediately assume
you've committed a crime.

I don't rest.
I stall.
I pause like a browser tab that refuses to load,
fans screaming,
cursor frozen,
everything overheating in the background.

My body might stop moving.
Nothing powers down.

Rest isn't a luxury.
It's not self-care.
It's not a cozy little reward you earn for being
productive enough.

Rest is a trap.
The second I stop,
everything I've been outrunning catches up.
Thoughts show up like debt collectors who finally
found my address.

Memories start tapping on the glass.
My nervous system leans forward like,
"Oh good. You're still. Now we can talk."

Absolutely fucking not.

Stillness Is Not Neutral

People love flattering explanations.

"You're driven."
"You're type A."
"You just don't know how to relax."

That's adorable.

I don't avoid rest because I love productivity.
I avoid rest because stillness feels unsafe.

When I slow down, my body panics.
Not metaphorically, physically.
Heart racing.
Chest tight.
Thoughts sprinting like they're late for a train.

My brain immediately starts interrogating me:
"Why are we stopping?"
"What did we forget?"
"What's about to go wrong?"

Because in my body's memory, stillness was never safe.
Stillness meant waiting.

Waiting to be noticed.
Waiting for the next blow.
Waiting for the punishment to drop.
Waiting for the floor to disappear.

So now rest feels like standing in enemy territory
without armor.

Hard pass.

Busy Is Safer Than Quiet

When I'm busy, I'm useful.
When I'm busy, I'm distracted.
When I'm busy, nothing terrible can sneak up on me
because I'm already braced for impact.

Busy feeds my anxiety something to chew on.
Busy drowns out the past.
Busy feels like control.

Quiet is where everything lives.
So rest doesn't feel calming,
it feels like vulnerability with no exit strategy.

I sit down and my chest tightens.
I lie down and my thoughts sprint.
I take a day off and my nervous system screams like I
just committed a felony.

You're falling behind.
You're wasting time.
You should be doing something.

What if something goes wrong while you're not paying attention?

Rest turns into interrogation.

Hypervigilance Doesn't Clock Out

I can be physically horizontal and still on full emotional patrol.
My body is still.
My brain is pacing like a feral animal trapped in a too small enclosure.
And God help me if rest actually starts to work.

If I feel even a flicker of calm, my system panics:
This is how people get hurt.
Peace feels suspicious.
Calm feels temporary.
Stillness feels like tempting fate.

So I sabotage it.
I scroll.
I clean something that doesn't need cleaning.
I start a project I didn't plan.
I manufacture urgency out of thin air because urgency feels familiar.

Rest is quiet.
Quiet is when shit used to happen.

Rest Doesn't Feel Relaxing, It Feels Guilty

Rest doesn't make me feel relaxed.

It makes me feel guilty.
Like I'm behind.
Like I'm lazy.
Like I'm disappointing an invisible jury that never adjourns.

If I'm not producing,
improving,
fixing,
or at least preparing to do one of those things,
my brain starts screaming that I'm wasting time and ruining everything.

So even when I "rest," I'm still working.
Mentally rehearsing.
Mentally apologizing.
Mentally punishing myself for stopping.
Rest becomes another task I'm failing at.

I Learned to Confuse Exhaustion with Safety

Here's the fucked-up math my nervous system runs:
As long as I'm tired, I'm trying.
As long as I'm drained, I'm earning my place.
As long as I'm depleted, no one can accuse me of slacking.

Rest feels morally wrong.
Like I haven't suffered enough yet to deserve it.
Like someone's going to catch me not struggling and revoke my right to exist.
So I stay tired on purpose.
I wear burnout like proof of character.

I treat rest like a suspicious stranger knocking on the door at night.

People say, "You need to slow down."
What I hear is, "You need to let your guard down."

No!

Control Is Oxygen

Rest isn't just stopping activity.
It's stopping vigilance.
And vigilance kept me alive.

Rest asks me to give up control.
Control feels like oxygen.
You don't casually give that up.

You hoard it.
You cling to it.
You choke on it if you have to.

And the cruel irony?
I'm exhausted because I won't rest.
I won't rest because I'm exhausted.
It's a closed loop of bullshit.

"You're Safe Now" is a Sentence My Body Doesn't Understand

People love to say, "You're safe now."
Cool.
My body does not believe you.

Safety isn't a concept.
It's a pattern.

And my body learned a different one.

One where staying alert mattered.
One where slowing down came with consequences.
One where rest was never free.

So no, this isn't about balance.
It's not about naps, meditation, or listening to your
body like it's a trustworthy narrator.

Sometimes your body is a trauma gremlin with a
megaphone.
Sometimes rest doesn't feel restorative.
Sometimes it feels like a threat you don't have the tools
to disarm.

Rest feels forbidden because once, stopping was not an
option.
And my nervous system hasn't gotten the memo that
the war is over…
especially when it still thinks I'm needed on watch.

So I keep moving.
I keep going.
I keep myself tired enough that rest never gets the
chance to betray me.

Not because I want to live like this.
But because my body still thinks stillness is how you
get hurt.

And honestly?
I don't know how to stop yet.

Chapter 14
Dissociation Is Not "Zoning Out"

This is not daydreaming.
This is an emergency exit.

People hear dissociation and think:
"Oh, like when I stare out the window in a meeting?"

No.
That's boredom.

Dissociation is your brain slamming the eject button because reality got too loud, too close, too much, and there was no other way out.

Zoning out is a coffee break.
Dissociation is a fire escape.
You don't drift.
You disappear.

When Your Brain Leaves the Room without You

Dissociation doesn't feel like relaxation.

It feels like:
- Watching your life through thick glass.
- Hearing your own voice sound fake and far away.
- Moving your body like it belongs to someone else.
- Time skipping like a scratched DVD.
- Knowing you're "here" but not in it.

You're conscious.
You're functioning.

You're absolutely not present.
Your brain didn't check with you.

It just said, "Nope. We're not doing this.

This Is a Survival Feature, Not a Personality Quirk

Let's be clear:
Dissociation exists because it worked.

When fighting wasn't safe.
When fleeing wasn't possible.
When staying present would've broken you.

So your brain did the only thing it could:
It left.

Not forever.
Just enough.

Enough to get through it.
Enough to keep you alive.
Enough to make the unbearable…bearable-ish.

Congratulations.
You survived.

Now enjoy the long-term subscription.

The Many Flavors of Not Being Here

Dissociation isn't one thing.
It's a sampler platter.

Sometimes it's mild:
You feel foggy.
Flat.
Disconnected.
Like someone turned the saturation down on reality.

Sometimes it's aggressive:
You lose chunks of time.
You don't recognize yourself.
Your reflection looks like a stranger who owes you
money.

Sometimes it's sneaky:
You're doing dishes.
Driving.
Working.
Answering emails.
Fully operational…no memory of any of it afterward.

Sometimes it's terrifying:
Your body feels unreal.
The world feels fake.
You're convinced you're losing your mind while
technically still paying bills.

Fun times.

"But You Look Fine" Is the Point

Of course I look fine.
Dissociation is a silent response.
No crying.
No screaming.
No visible meltdown.
Just absence.

Which is why it gets missed.
Dismissed.
Misunderstood.
People don't panic when you dissociate.
They just think you're cold.
Checked out.
Lazy.
Not trying hard enough.

Meanwhile, your brain is running a covert evacuation
drill like its saving civilians from a burning building.

It's Not Avoidance. It's Containment.

Dissociation isn't about refusing to deal with feelings.
It's about not having the capacity to feel them safely.

When emotions hit at nuclear levels,
dissociation becomes a containment unit.

Your brain says:
"We can't process this right now.
We'll store it.
Somewhere.
We'll deal with it later."

Spoiler:
Later always comes with interest.

The Cost of Leaving Your Body Repeatedly

Dissociation fractures continuity.
You lose memory.
You lose time.
You lose a clean sense of self.
You don't feel like a whole person.

You feel like a rotating cast of versions,
none of whom fully remember what the others did.
You struggle with identity because presence was never
consistent enough to build one.

And people wonder why you feel disconnected from
your own life.

The Shame Layer

Dissociation comes with guilt.

You feel lazy.
Unproductive.
"Not engaged."

You judge yourself for not being present enough.
For missing things.
For forgetting conversations,
commitments,
whole emotional stretches of your life.

You apologize constantly for things you don't
remember doing.
And no one tells you that dissociation isn't a moral
failure.

It's a nervous system choosing survival.

When Dissociation Becomes the Default Setting

Here's where it gets extra fucked up:
After enough trauma, dissociation stops being a
response.
It becomes a baseline.
You don't dissociate during stress anymore.

You dissociate during calm.
Quiet feels unsafe.
Stillness feels exposed.
Presence feels like a trap.

So you float.
Always a little removed.
Always half-gone.

People call it depression.
Or avoidance.
Or detachment.

It's not.

It's your brain refusing to come fully back online
because it remembers what happened last time.

No, You're Not Crazy

Dissociation can feel like losing your mind.
You question reality.
You question yourself.
You worry you're "too far gone."
You're not.

You're doing exactly what a human brain does when it
learned early that staying fully present was dangerous.

This isn't weakness.
It's pattern recognition.

There Is No Clean Fix

Sometimes dissociation fades.
Sometimes it doesn't.
Sometimes it shifts forms.
Sometimes it shows up when you least expect it and
ruins your day like an uninvited guest who eats all your
snacks and leaves emotional debris.

There is no neat ending where you suddenly feel
embodied and safe and real all the time.
There is just negotiation.
And awareness.
And the slow, irritating realization that your brain kept
you alive in the only way it knew how, and now you're
stuck managing the side effects.

Dissociation is not zoning out.
It's not being dramatic.
It's not lack of effort.
It's what happens when your brain decides presence is
too risky and absence is safer.

If you disappear inside yourself sometimes.
If you feel unreal, detached, foggy, or far away.
If your memory feels like Swiss cheese and your sense
of self feels glitchy.
You're not broken.
You're adapted.
And adaptation, unfortunately, doesn't come with an
off switch.

Sometimes survival means leaving the room.
And learning how to live with that is its own quiet,
exhausting battle.

Chapter 15
Fantasizing About Disappearing Without Dying

I don't want to die.
I want to stop being perceived.

Let's clear this up immediately so no one panics and hands me a hotline like a party favor:

I don't want to die.
I want to vanish.

Different fantasy.
Different flavor of desperation.

Death is loud.
Final.
Permanent.

Disappearing is quiet.
Reversible.
Polite.

It's the urge to step out of existence without causing a scene or paperwork.

The Fantasy Is Not Violence. It's Silence.

The fantasy isn't blood or bridges or goodbye notes.

It's:
- Changing my name.
- Leaving my phone behind.
- Becoming unreachable.
- No one needing anything.

- No one asking questions.
- No one expecting replies.

Just peace via absence.
A spiritual Irish goodbye.

This Is What Burnout Sounds Like When It Learns Big Words

People call this passive suicidal ideation and immediately ruin it by misunderstanding the assignment.

Because this isn't about wanting life to end.
It's about wanting responsibility to end.

You don't fantasize about disappearing because you hate living.
You fantasize about disappearing because living has turned into unpaid labor with no PTO.

Emails.
Bills.
People's feelings.
Your own feelings.
Maintenance.
Maintenance.
Maintenance.

You don't want to stop breathing.
You want to stop being on call.

I Want a Witness Protection Program for the Overwhelmed

I want a government-funded program where they go:

"Yeah. You're cooked.
Here's a new identity.
Go sit by a lake.
No one can ask anything of you for six months."

No trauma processing.
No healing.
No personal growth.
Just absence.

This Is a Trauma Response, Not a Plot Twist

Disappearing fantasies show up when:
- Asking for help didn't help.
- Rest wasn't allowed.
- Needs were punished.
- Presence felt unsafe.
- Being seen cost too much.

When being visible hurt, your brain learned the solution
was not being here.
Not dead.
Just…offstage.

The Fantasy Is Control without Carnage

Here's the uncomfortable part:
Disappearing fantasies feel safe.
No one gets hurt.
No one mourns.
No one panics.
No one stages an intervention.
You just slip out the back door and let the world run
without you for a while.

It's control without destruction.
Which is why the fantasy sticks.

"Must Be Nice to Run Away From Your Problems."
Shut Up

People love to reduce this to escapism.
As if this is about avoiding consequences.

It's not.
It's about avoiding constant exposure.
Being perceived.
Being required.
Being needed.
Being managed.
Being evaluated.

You don't want to escape life.
You want life to stop touching you.

This Is What Happens When Rest Feels Unsafe

If rest ever meant:
- Criticism
- Danger
- Guilt
- Punishment
- Abandonment

Then disappearing feels like the only form of rest that won't be interrupted.
You can't relax if someone might knock.
So you fantasize about leaving the building entirely.

The Guilt Layer (Because There's Always Guilt)

You feel guilty for thinking this.
Because:
- You have people who love you.
- You have responsibilities.
- You're "needed."

So the fantasy becomes shame-soaked.

You tell yourself you're selfish.
Immature.
Ungrateful.

But what you actually are is exhausted beyond
language.

You Don't Want to Be Missed. You Want to Be Unreachable.

That's the difference people don't get.
You're not fantasizing about absence being noticed.
You're fantasizing about absence being undetected.
No search parties.
No "where did they go?"
No legacy.
Just quiet.

This Is the Mind's Compromise with Survival

Fantasizing about disappearing is often how people
avoid suicidal thoughts.
It's the brain saying:
"I can't keep doing this like this, but I also don't want
to die."
So it invents a third option.

A mental fire exit.
Not an action plan.
Not intent.
A pressure valve.

There Is No Resolution Here

I'm not going to tell you this means you secretly want
to die.
You don't.

I'm not going to tell you it's a red flag that needs
immediate fixing.
It's not.

I'm not going to tell you how to ground yourself.
You already know the techniques.

They don't touch this.
This isn't panic.
It's fatigue.
Existential, cellular, bone-deep fatigue.

If you fantasize about disappearing…
About changing your name, your face, your life…
About being unreachable without being dead…
You are not broken.
You are not a risk.
You are not dramatic.
You are overwhelmed in a world that refuses to slow
down or soften.

You don't want to end your life.
You want your life to stop asking so much of you.

And no, there's no happy ending here.

Just honesty.

Sometimes the most comforting thought is not death.
It's silence.

And the fantasy of finally,
mercifully,
being left the fuck alone.

Part III: When Your Brain Starts Negotiating With Death

Chapter 16
Suicidal Ideation: When Your Brain Suggests Death Like it's a Reasonable Option

Let's talk about the thought you're afraid to say out loud because you're worried it will somehow summon a grippy-sock vacation or a wellness check you did not order.

There's a version of this thought people are comfortable with.

It sounds like:
"I'm overwhelmed."
"I'm burned out."
"I'm tired."

Sure.
Sometimes that's true.

But then there's the other version.
The one that makes rooms go quiet.
The one that gets you watched differently.

The thought that sounds like:
"I don't want to be here."
Not "I want to die."
Not "I have a plan."
Just…
"I'm done being conscious."

And that's the part nobody prepares you for.

Suicidal ideation doesn't always arrive screaming.
Sometimes it slides in calmly.
Casually.

Like a suggestion.
Like your brain leaning over mid-chaos and saying,
"Okay, but what if we just…didn't exist?"

Not urgent.
Not dramatic.

With the same tone it uses to suggest ordering takeout.

Your brain doesn't present death like a tragedy.
It presents it like a solution.
A full stop.
A clean exit.
A way to make the noise stop without having to explain
yourself to anyone.

And for a second,
sometimes longer than a second,
it makes sense.

That's what scares people.

They imagine suicidal thoughts as screaming despair.
They don't picture them arriving calmly,
logically,
wrapped in relief.
Like a sales pitch.
Like an option on the table.

Your brain doesn't say, "I want to die."
It says, "I don't want to keep doing this."

Those are very different sentences.

Suicidal Ideation Isn't Always Dramatic

Hollywood lied.

Suicidal ideation is not always sobbing on the floor
with swelling violins and rain dramatically hitting the
window.

Sometimes it's:
Standing in the shower wondering how long you could
just…stay there.
Driving and thinking, "If something happened, I
wouldn't fight it."
Wishing you could fall asleep and not wake up, but in a
chill, not-a-big-deal way.
Feeling irritated that you have to keep existing
tomorrow.

It's not loud.
It's not urgent.
It's not even always emotional.
Sometimes it's logistical.

Like your brain scrolling through exits without intent,
just curiosity.

And because that scares the shit out of people,
we pretend it doesn't exist.

This Is Not Always About Wanting to Die

Here's what people don't understand unless they've
lived it:
Most suicidal ideation isn't about death.
It's about relief.

Relief from:
- The noise.
- The panic.
- The exhaustion.
- The shame.
- The endless effort of staying functional in a world that feels hostile, loud, and relentless.

You don't want to be dead.
You want the pressure off your chest.
You want one goddamn day where being alive doesn't feel like a performance review.
You want rest that actually works.

But because our emotional vocabulary is trash, everything gets flattened into binaries:

Alive or dead.
Fine or crisis.
Safe or danger.

There is no category for:
"I am exhausted in a way sleep will not fix."
So your brain grabs the biggest off-switch it can imagine.
Not because it's correct.
Because it's desperate.

Suicidal ideation shows up when coping mechanisms are maxed out.
When distraction stops working.
When dissociation gets tired.
When anxiety, depression, burnout, and shame pile on at once and your brain starts flipping through emergency exits.

It's not drama.
It's protection.

The Shame Layer (Because ... Shame)

The thought appears.
Then immediately comes the guilt.
"What kind of person thinks this?"
"Other people have it worse."
"I should be grateful."
"This means something is seriously wrong with me."

Congratulations.

Now you're suicidal and self-loathing.
Excellent teamwork.

So you bury it.
You don't say it out loud because you don't want to
scare anyone.
You don't want to be watched.
You don't want to be monitored.
You don't want to become a liability.
So you keep it quiet.

You live with a brain that occasionally suggests death
like it's a reasonable backup plan,
and you go about your day like this is fine.

You cook dinner.
You answer texts.
You laugh at memes.
You have a full internal debate about whether
continuing to exist is worth the effort,
and then you still show up to shit.
That's the part people don't get.

Suicidal ideation doesn't always look like giving up.
Sometimes it looks like enduring.
White-knuckling through days while your brain
casually floats the idea of not having to do this
anymore.

When Your Brain Starts Negotiating

Here's where it gets quietly slippery.
Your brain starts bargaining with you.
Not "do it now."
Just…
"You don't have to decide today."
"Just keep it as an option."
"It's good to have an exit."

It feels oddly calming.
Like knowing there's a fire escape.
But once your brain labels death as an option, it will
keep offering it during moments of stress, even when
you don't want it.

That doesn't make you broken.
It means your brain learned a shortcut it shouldn't have.

Thoughts Are Not Intent

This matters.

Thoughts are not commands.
Thoughts are not plans.
Thoughts are not destiny.

Your brain produces garbage all day long.
You don't act on every angry thought.
You don't obey every anxious one.

You don't believe every intrusive image.
Suicidal thoughts deserve the same skepticism.

Having the thought does not mean you want to die.
Having the thought does not mean you're going to act.
Having the thought means your system is overloaded.

That's it.

When you're Afraid of Your Own Brain

One of the most isolating parts of suicidal ideation is
becoming afraid of yourself.
You start monitoring your thoughts like:
"Is this escalating?"
"Am I okay?"
"What if I lose control?"

That fear can be as exhausting as the thought itself.

Here's something people don't say enough:
People who are scared by suicidal thoughts are usually
the ones who want to live.

Fear is protective.
Concern is attachment.
The thought scares you because you care.
But it hums in the background anyway.
Not loud enough to stop you.
Not quiet enough to ignore.

What if this stress tips me?
What if this loss pushes me?
What if I don't notice until it's bad again?

You don't catastrophize.
You remember.

Why We Don't Talk About This (And Why That's a Problem)

We treat suicidal thoughts like a forbidden subject.
Like naming them will make them stronger.
So people suffer silently.
They assume they're alone.
They assume everyone else is coping better.
They're not.

Suicidal ideation is far more common than anyone wants to admit, especially among people who are high-functioning, funny, responsible, and absolutely exhausted.

Silence doesn't keep people safe.
It just keeps them alone with their worst thoughts.

Continuing Without Hope

This is not a pep talk.
This is not a tidy bow.
This is not where everything suddenly feels manageable.

Sometimes your brain suggests death not because life is worthless, but because continuing to live feels like an unbearable amount of work.

And you keep going anyway.

Not heroically.
Not inspirationally.

Just stubbornly.

One hour.
One day.
One breath at a time.

While your mind argues with itself in the background.

Having these thoughts doesn't make you a lost cause.
It makes you human under more weight than one
nervous system was ever meant to hold.

Chapter 17
Self-Harm: When Pain Feels Like Control (And Control Feels like Oxygen)

Let's rip the bandage off immediately:
Self-harm is not about attention.
It's not about drama.
It's not about wanting to die.

If it were about death, it would be quieter.
Shorter.
More decisive.

Self-harm is about staying.
Staying present.
Staying in your body.
Staying upright when everything inside you is screaming.

Self-harm is about regulation.
And if that sentence makes you flinch,
Congratulations, you've been fed a lot of bullshit.

Why Pain Can Feel Like Relief (Unfortunately)

When your internal world is chaos, panic screaming, thoughts racing, and emotions colliding like feral cats in a dryer, pain does something very specific:
It narrows the focus.

Pain says, "Here. This. One thing."
It cuts through numbness.
It interrupts dissociation.
It drags you back into your body when you've floated too far away to function.

Not because pain is enjoyable,
kill that myth immediately,
but because it's reliable.
Predictable.
Immediate.
It does what it promises.

When your brain is static and noise and nothing lands,
pain cuts through like a hard reset.

For a moment, you feel real.
That doesn't make it healthy.
It makes it effective.
And effectiveness is why it's reinforcing.

Control in a World That Took It from You

Control is the currency here.
For a lot of people, self-harm begins in environments
where control was scarce or stolen outright,
where feelings were ignored,
bodies weren't fully yours,
needs were minimized,
and nothing felt negotiable.
So you found a lever.

This pain is chosen.
This pain has rules.
This pain starts and stops when you decide.

In a life that feels like it's happening to you,
that tiny pocket of control can feel like oxygen.
You don't need a lot.
You just need enough to breathe.
People assume self-harm is impulsive.
Often it's the opposite.

It's deliberate.
Calculated.
A way to reclaim agency when everything else feels
owned by someone, or something, else.

Again: not an endorsement.
An explanation.

"Why Would You Do That to Yourself?"

Because emotional pain is invisible and routinely
invalidated.
Because people debate feelings but understand injuries.
Because when you say, I'm hurting, people ask
questions.
When you bleed, they pay attention.

Because when emotions are too big,
too chaotic,
too wordless,
pain translates them into something legible.
Something with edges.
Something you can point to and say, "There. That's it."

Pain doesn't gaslight you.
Pain doesn't argue.
Pain shows up, does its job, and shuts up.

And when numbness has eaten everything else,
pain can make you feel alive again.

That doesn't make you broken.
It makes you desperate for relief.

The Part Nobody Wants to Admit

It works.
For a minute.

The relief is real.
The grounding is real.
The sense of control is real.
Your nervous system goes,
"Oh thank God. Something makes sense again."

And then,
like every coping strategy born in crisis,
it turns on you.

The relief fades.
The shame spikes.
The secrecy thickens.

Now you're not just overwhelmed, you're hiding.

You carry a private war under your clothes and inside
your head.
You manage other people's perceptions while
managing your own urges.

You learn what you can and can't say,
who you can and can't trust,
how much of yourself is allowed to exist out loud.

You're not doing it because you like hurting yourself.
You're doing it because you don't know how else to
regulate a system that never learned how to come back
down.

The Shame Spiral (Featuring Everyone's Opinions)

Self-harm comes preloaded with shame.
People react with horror.
Judgment.
Anger.
Ultimatums.
"Why would you do this to people who love you?"

Which is wild, considering you're doing it because
you're in pain,
not because you're auditioning for moral failure.

Shame does not stop self-harm.
It fuels it.

The more disgusting you feel, the more you want relief.
The more relief you get, the worse you feel afterward.

Congratulations.

You're trapped in a loop.

The Aftermath Nobody Warns You About

Self-harm rarely ends with relief alone.
It ends with guilt.
Embarrassment.
Fear of being found out.
The promise to "never do it again."
The urge returning anyway.

You don't feel proud.
You feel conflicted.
You hate that it helped.
You hate that you needed it.

You hate yourself for both.
And then you swear you'll stop…
until the next time your nervous system is on fire and
nothing else works fast enough.

This is not a willpower issue.

Say it again:
This is not a willpower issue.

You cannot shame yourself into stopping.
You cannot bully yourself into safety.
You cannot hate yourself into regulation.

If "just don't" worked, you would have already done
that.

This is coping.

Maladaptive coping, yes, but coping nonetheless.

You learned it because it worked when your options
were limited.

The Contradiction That Breaks People's Brains

Yes, self-harm can coexist with wanting to live.
That contradiction fries people's circuits.
They can't understand how someone could hurt
themselves and still want to be here.
But that's exactly the point.

Self-harm is often an attempt to stay alive without
completely falling apart.

A pressure-release valve.

A grounding technique.
A way to feel something when numbness has eaten
everything else.

It doesn't mean you're weak.
It means your system was overwhelmed and
improvised.
Improvisation under threat is messy.

There Is No Neat Ending Here

There's no montage where healthier coping skills arrive
with better lighting and a supportive soundtrack.

Sometimes it stops.
Sometimes it shifts.
Sometimes it comes back when things get unbearable
again.

That doesn't make you a failure.

It makes you someone who learned how to survive in
an environment where control was scarce and pain was
familiar.

This isn't about scaring you straight or shaming you
into compliance.

It's here to say the quiet part out loud:
Self-harm isn't about death.
It's about regulation.
It's about control.
It's about staying functional when everything inside
you is screaming.

Surviving it doesn't make you noble or cured.

It makes you honest about the lengths a human nervous system will go to in order to keep breathing.

Chapter 18
Suicide Attempts: The Stories Nobody Knows What to Do With After You Survive

Surviving a suicide attempt does not come with a parade.

There are no balloons.
No medals.
No card that says, "Great job not dying!"

Mostly, there's silence.
Awkward silence.
Uncomfortable silence.

The kind where people don't know whether to hug you,
avoid you,
or pretend it never happened.

So let's talk about the part nobody prepares you for:

Living after you didn't die.

Survival Is Not Redemption

Everyone thinks there's a script for this.
They imagine you waking up grateful.
Reborn.
Enlightened.
Ready to seize life like a phoenix with a therapist and a
vision board.

That is not what happens.
What happens is confusion.
What happens is embarrassment.

What happens is exhaustion so deep you don't know
where to put it.

Surviving doesn't make you inspirational.
It makes you complicated.

You don't come back triumphant.
You come back carrying memory.
And memory is heavy.

You didn't suddenly become "fixed."
You just became alive with consequences,
physical ones,
emotional ones,
social ones.

Sometimes surviving doesn't even mean you want to
live.

Sometimes it just means you didn't die.

There's a difference.

The Immediate Aftermath: Everyone Watching You Breathe

Right after, there's often a strange calm.
Not peace, more like emotional whiplash.

You might feel:
- Embarrassed.
- Ashamed.
- Guilty for hurting people.
- Relieved it didn't work.
- Angry that it didn't work.
- Terrified it might happen again.

Sometimes all at once.
Sometimes on a rotating schedule like emotional
whack-a-mole.

And then there are other people.

People who suddenly look at you like:
You're fragile glass.
You're radioactive.
You owe them reassurance.
You owe them survival forever now.

Your pain becomes public property.
Your existence becomes monitored.
You're alive, but now you're marked.
You can feel it.
The recalibration.
The mental footnote next to your name.
The unspoken fragile label hovering in the room.

"But You're Still Here!" (Yes. That's the Point.)

People say things like:
"Aren't you glad you're alive?"
"Everything happens for a reason."
"It made you stronger."

Listen carefully.

Being alive does not automatically feel like a gift.
Surviving does not immediately feel good.
Sometimes it just feels like unfinished business you
didn't ask for.

You didn't attempt because you wanted attention.
You didn't attempt because you were weak.

You attempted because, in that moment, your pain
outweighed your ability to cope.

Survival does not erase that truth.
And now you're expected to make everyone else
comfortable with the fact that you didn't die.

The Fear No One Sees

One of the most isolating parts of surviving is the fear
that comes after.

Not fear of death.
Fear of yourself.

You start thinking:
"What if I get that bad again?"
"What if I can't trust my own mind?"
"What if next time I don't stop?"

That fear doesn't mean you want to die.
It means you understand how close the edge actually is.
And that knowledge doesn't go away just because you
survived.

Survival Is Not a Clean Slate

Everyone assumes the crisis is over because you're still
breathing.
They don't see the aftermath.
The hypervigilance.
The way your brain now knows exactly how thin the
line is.
The way stress hits harder because you've already seen
where it can lead.

Survival is not a reset button.
It's a scar people want you to cover politely.
And God help you if you try to talk about it honestly.

If you're too sad, people panic.
If you joke, people recoil.
If you're matter-of-fact, people think you're cold.
If you're still struggling, people get uncomfortable.

There is no correct tone for having survived.

Dark humor becomes your pressure valve,
not because it's funny,
but because it's the only socially acceptable way to
acknowledge something this fucked without everyone
bolting for the exits.

And even then:
Laugh too hard and you're "minimizing."
Laugh at the wrong moment and you're "concerning."
Don't laugh and you're "not coping well."

So you learn to manage other people's reactions to your
survival while still managing the fallout inside your
own head.

Survivor Shame Is a Special Kind of Hell

Survivor shame is brutal.
Shame for scaring people.
Shame for needing help.
Shame for not being "better" now.
Shame for still hurting.

It whispers:
"You should be grateful."

"You don't get to struggle anymore."
"You already used your crisis card."

That is bullshit.

Surviving does not mean you forfeit the right to still
hurt.
It does not mean you owe the world perfection.
It does not mean your mental health struggles are
invalid now.

It means you lived.
That's it.

When People Try to Turn You into a Lesson

There is a specific circle of hell reserved for being
turned into inspiration porn.

"You're so strong."
"You're an inspiration."
"Everything happens for a reason."

No.

You survived something that almost killed you.

You're allowed to be angry about that.
You're allowed to be tired.
You're allowed to not package it into a moral takeaway.

Survival is not always brave.

Sometimes it's stubborn.
Sometimes it's resentful.

Sometimes it's just refusing to die out of spite.
That still counts.

Living after an Attempt Is Complicated

There will be days you forget it happened.
There will be days it feels like it happened yesterday.

Triggers appear out of nowhere.
Anniversaries sneak up on you.
Your body remembers before your brain does.

This doesn't mean you're failing.
It means your nervous system remembers how close the
edge was.
And that memory doesn't disappear just because you're
still here.

The Truth No One Likes to Say

Surviving a suicide attempt doesn't fix your life.
It complicates it.

It hands you a story people don't know how to hold
and asks you to keep living anyway,
without instructions,
without applause,
without certainty.

You didn't fail at dying.
You didn't succeed at living.
You landed in the middle.
Where everything is heavier.
Where nothing is simple.
Where people want closure and you're still bleeding
internally.

And you keep going.

Not because you're healed.
Not because everything suddenly makes sense.
But because somehow, against all odds, expectations,
and neat narratives, you're still here.
Carrying a story the world doesn't know what to do
with.
Learning how to exist with it one unglamorous, deeply
human day at a time.

That's not inspirational.
It's just the truth.

Chapter 19
The Aftermath: Living after the Worst Thing Didn't Kill You (Rude)

Nobody prepares you for the after.
Not after the breakdown.
Not after the attempt.
Not after the hospitalization,
the confession,
the night you didn't think you'd see morning.

Everyone talks about prevention.
No one talks about the hangover.

Surviving doesn't roll credits.
It drops you back into your life with a headache,
a receipt,
and the unsettling realization that you're still expected
to function.

You wake up like,
"Excuse me? I was under the impression this was the
end of the episode."

But no.
The season continues.

Same cast.
Same responsibilities.
Same fucking bills.

Survival is not cinematic.
There's no swelling music.
No clean reset.
No dramatic clarity where you emerge wiser and
glowing like a trauma butterfly.

You wake up sore.
Embarrassed.
Still depressed.
Still anxious.
Still you.
Just with more paperwork and fewer illusions.

You lived.
Now what.

Here's the part that feels illegal to say out loud:
Sometimes surviving feels worse than dying would
have.
Not because you want to die,
but because now you have to carry the memory of how
close you came.

You remember:
- The exact moment things tipped.
- The thought that scared you.
- The calm that wasn't peace.
- The fear afterward.

And then the world goes,
"Anyway, how's work?"
Rude.

Relief, Regret, Rage, Gratitude
Pick Three (Rotating)

The emotional cocktail post-crisis is unhinged.

You might feel relieved you're alive.
Furious you're still here.
Ashamed you scared people.
Guilty for not being "grateful enough."

Terrified of your own brain.
Weirdly numb.
Sometimes all of that before lunch.

People want a single emotion.
They want a headline.
You get a cyclone.

The Surveillance Phase

After a crisis, suddenly everyone is watching.
"How are you feeling?"
"Are you okay?"
"Promise you'll call if…"

Their concern is real.
So is your irritation.

You don't want to be babysat.
You don't want to be fragile glass.
You don't want your pain to become a group project.

You survived.
You didn't sign up to be monitored like a haunted
artifact.
And yet,
some part of you is grateful someone is paying attention
now.

That contradiction will haunt you for a while.

When People Want Closure and You Want Quiet

People crave resolution.
They want:
- A reason.
- A lesson.
- A takeaway.
- A redemption.

You want:
- Space.
- Normalcy.
- Fewer questions.
- Less eye contact.

You don't owe anyone an explanation tidy enough to soothe their discomfort.
You don't have to turn your worst moment into a *TED Talk*.

Sometimes the only honest explanation is:
"I was overwhelmed and didn't see another way."

That's not a failure.
That's the truth.

You Know Too Much Now

Surviving doesn't make you feel lucky.
It makes you feel exposed.

You know how close the edge actually is.
You know how quickly your brain can flip the table and start pitching exits.
You know what your breaking point smells like, sounds like,

And feels like in your body.

That knowledge doesn't leave.
It sets up shop.

The aftermath is living with the awareness that you are
capable of falling that far,
and still being expected to answer emails politely.

You don't feel reborn.
You feel returned to sender.

People assume the worst is over because you're upright.
They don't see the hypervigilance.
The flinch response.
The way your body still braces for disaster even on
quiet days.

"Normal" feels fake now.
You're not the same person,
but you're not a new one either.

You're some feral in-between creature trying to exist
without constantly checking for exits.

The Body Keeps the Memory (Rude, Again)

Your nervous system does not forget.
You might notice:
- Panic spikes for no obvious reason.
- Nightmares.
- Dissociation.
- Startle responses.
- Sudden exhaustion.

This doesn't mean you're regressing.

It means your body learned how close the edge was and
is now overcorrecting like a panicked intern with access
to all the alarms.

Your body is not sabotaging you.
It's trying (poorly) to keep you alive.

The Pressure to Be "Better Now"

There's an unspoken expectation after survival:
"Okay, you lived. Can we all move on?"

You feel pressure to:
- Perform wellness.
- Downplay how bad it still is.
- Avoid "going there" again.
- Prove you're safe now.

Here's the truth nobody likes:
Healing after crisis is not linear, polite, or fast.
You don't reset to factory settings.
You recalibrate with a system that's been shaken.

You're allowed to still struggle.
You're allowed to need help.
You're allowed to not be inspirational.

When the Thoughts Come Back (And You Panic About That)

This matters:
Having dark thoughts after a crisis does not mean
you're doomed to repeat it.

Thoughts returning are not equal to intent returning.

Your brain learned a pathway under extreme stress.
It may revisit it automatically.
That's scary.
It's also common.

The difference now?
You notice sooner.
You take it more seriously.
You're more willing to reach out.
That's not weakness.
That's growth with scars.

The Grief Nobody Mentions

There's grief after survival.

Grief for:
- The version of you before everything shattered.
- The illusion of being "fine."
- The belief you could outwork pain.
- The time you lost to recovery.

Survival costs something.
Pretending it doesn't only makes the bill worse later.

You Don't Owe the World Impossible Promises

People ask for promises.
"Promise you'll never do that again."
"Promise you'll tell me if you feel like that."

You can promise effort.
You can promise honesty.
You can promise to try.

You cannot promise perfection.

Anyone who demands that is prioritizing their comfort
over your reality.

Living Is the Hard Part

Surviving is an event.
Living is the work.
It's messy.
Boring.
Uneven.
Sometimes deeply unfair.

You live out of habit.
Out of stubbornness.
Out of spite sometimes.
You live because you're already here and leaving
would cause paperwork you don't have the energy for.

The aftermath isn't about triumph.
It's about coexistence.
Coexisting with memories that don't ask permission.
With a body that remembers even when you don't want
it to.
With a brain that now knows how bad it can get,
and keeps that file handy.

You lived through something that should have ended
you,
and now you have to live after it,
which is somehow harder and far less celebrated.

If that feels unfair?
Yeah.
It kind of is.

You don't need to be grateful.

You don't need to be fixed.
You don't need to be brave.
You just need to keep choosing to exist.

Even feral.
Even exhausted.
Even unsure.

Especially then.

Part IV:
Staying Alive (Against Your Will)

Chapter 20
Resenting People Who Threaten Suicide for Attention

This is where the judgement starts.
Because the moment you say this out loud, people hear cruelty.
They hear lack of compassion.
They hear you punching down.

That's not what this is.
This is exhaustion.

You're Not Mad at Pain. You're Mad at the Theater around It.

Let's be precise.
You're not angry that someone is hurting.
You're angry at the performance of it.
The vague posts.
The countdown texts.
The "don't worry about me" followed by immediate escalation.
The crisis as leverage.

It hits a nerve because you know what real danger looks like,
and this isn't it.

Not the same way.

Your Body Knows the Difference before Your Values Catch Up

Your nervous system reacts first.
Because you've been there.

Because you've sat with the quiet, lethal certainty.
Because you know how invisible real risk can be.
So when someone uses suicidal language as a flare for attention,
your body goes rigid.

Not from judgment.
From recognition, and resentment.

It Feels like They're Using the Thing That Almost Killed You

Suicide isn't abstract to you.
It's not metaphor.
It's not language.
It's something that almost took your life,
or someone you loved.

So watching it get weaponized for reassurance, control, or validation, feels like sacrilege.

Like someone casually handling a loaded gun you once stared down.

You're Angry Because the System Responds Faster to Noise than Need

Here's the bitter truth:
Loud distress gets attention.
Persistent suffering gets ignored.

People who threaten get rushed care.
People who quietly deteriorate get missed.

You know this because you lived it.
So resentment builds, not toward the person,

but toward a system that rewards spectacle over sincerity.

You're Afraid to Say This Because It Sounds like Gatekeeping Pain

You don't want to be the person who decides whose pain counts.
You know pain is messy.
You know coping can look manipulative when it's desperate.
You know attention-seeking is often attachment-seeking in disguise.

You know all that.
And you're still angry.
Both can be true.

This Anger Is About Safety, Not Superiority

People assume resentment means you think you're "more legitimate."

That's not it.

You're angry because false alarms dilute urgency.
Because they make people cynical.
Because they teach responders to doubt.
And doubt kills quiet people.

That's the fear underneath the anger.

You're Also Mad Because You Never Got to Ask That Loudly

You didn't threaten.
You didn't broadcast.
You didn't make it dramatic.
You held it inside.
You minimized.
You nearly disappeared without anyone noticing.

So watching someone receive immediate care for behavior you were taught was unacceptable?

That hurts.

You Know Threatening Isn't the Same as Wanting to Die

Here's the nuance no one holds:
Some people threaten suicide because they don't know how else to say,
"I need you to stay."

That doesn't make them evil.
It makes them desperate and unskilled.
But it still has consequences.
And you're allowed to be angry about the impact.

You're allowed to Be Compassionate and Furious

Compassion doesn't require silence.
Empathy doesn't require self-erasure.
You can understand why someone does this and still resent how it distorts care, consumes resources, and re-traumatizes people who've lived on the edge.
Those emotions are not opposites.

People Want You to Be Nicer About This Than Reality Allows

They say:
"Any expression of suicidality should be taken seriously."

True.

They don't say:
"And it's okay if that seriousness costs survivors something."

But it does.

It costs you trust.
It costs you bandwidth.
It costs you the ability to feel safe around the language.

This Isn't a Call to Dismiss Anyone

Let's be clear:
This is not permission to ignore threats.
Not permission to decide who deserves help.
Not permission to minimize danger.

This is permission to name the resentment that builds when survival taught you how fragile the system really is.

I'm not going to tell you to soften this.
I'm not going to tell you to reframe it.
I'm not going to tell you you're wrong for feeling it.
This is just admitting that anger exists,
and pretending it doesn't just pushes it underground.

If you resent people who threaten suicide for
attention…
If it makes your chest tighten instead of your heart
open…
If you feel ashamed for thinking this way…

You're not heartless.

You're responding to a system that taught you real
danger is quiet,
help is inconsistent,
and spectacle gets prioritized over sustained suffering.

You can hold compassion and anger.
You can want people safe and want honesty about
impact.
You can care and be furious.

When you've lived near the edge,
watching the language of death get used as currency
does something to you,
and that reaction deserves to be named, not buried.

You're allowed to feel this.
And you're allowed to want a system that takes all pain
seriously.
Not just the loud kind.

Chapter 21
Resenting Children or Dependents for Being Your Reason to Stay

This is the thought you swallow immediately.
Because it sounds monstrous.
Because it sounds unloving.
Because it sounds like something you're not allowed to feel.

And yet…
There it is.

Love Didn't Ask to Be the Leash

You love them.
That's not the question.

The question is what happens when love becomes the only thing tethering you to life.
When staying alive stops being a choice and becomes an obligation with a face.

You don't resent them.
You resent the fact that your exit is no longer yours to contemplate,
even privately.

They Became the Final Argument

People say:
"But you have kids."
"They need you."
"Think about them."

As if your life is now a safety mechanism instead of a
human experience.
As if your pain is less relevant because someone
depends on you.

You didn't choose their existence to be used as a reason
you're not allowed to leave.

That happened to you.

Being Needed Is Not the Same as Being Held

Here's the ugly truth:
Being needed can feel suffocating when you're already
drowning.

Need is directional.
It pulls.
It demands.
It doesn't ask how you're doing.
You're allowed to want care toward you,
not just responsibility flowing out of you.

You're Afraid to Admit This Because It Sounds like You Regret Them

You don't.
You regret the position.
You regret that your existence became instrumental.
That your worth got reduced to what would happen if
you were gone.

You didn't stop loving them.
You stopped being allowed to consider yourself.

Resentment Grows Where There Is No Relief

You're exhausted.
And exhaustion breeds resentment when there's no off
switch.
No sick days from being the reason.
No pause button on responsibility.
No room to say, I can't carry this today.

So the resentment turns inward,
and then leaks sideways.
And then you hate yourself for it.

People Romanticize "Staying for Them"

They call it noble.
Selfless.
Beautiful.

They don't live inside the day-to-day reality of it.
They don't feel what it's like to wake up already
obligated to survive,
regardless of how you feel about being here.

They don't feel the quiet rage of knowing your pain
doesn't get to be terminal anymore, just managed.

You Miss When Staying Alive Was About You

This is the grief no one names.
You miss when your life was yours to negotiate with
yourself.
When the decision was internal.
When the stakes were terrifying, but personal.

Now the stakes are relational.

And that changes everything.

You're Afraid the Resentment Makes You Harmful

You worry:
If I admit this, does it mean I don't love them enough?
Does it mean I shouldn't be responsible for anyone?

No.

It means you're human under pressure.

Resentment doesn't equal harm.
Silencing it does.

You Can Love Someone and Hate the Weight They
Place on Survival

This is the nuance people refuse to hold:
Love and resentment are not opposites.
They coexist when responsibility outpaces capacity.

You can adore your child, partner, parent, pet,
and still hate that their dependence removes your
freedom to collapse.

That doesn't make you selfish.
It makes you honest about the cost.

You're allowed to Want Relief without Wanting
Escape

You don't want them gone.
You don't want to disappear.
You want the pressure to ease.
The weight to be shared.

The reason to stay to include you, not just them.

That desire doesn't threaten anyone.
It asks for help.

This Is What Happens When Support Is Moralized

When staying alive becomes a moral duty,
resentment follows.
Because morality doesn't provide rest.
It provides judgment.
You don't need more reasons.
You need more support.

No Shame Ritual. Just Naming the Reality.

I'm not going to tell you to be grateful.
I'm not going to tell you to reframe this as purpose.
I'm not going to tell you you're lucky to have a reason.

Sometimes a reason feels like a chain.
Naming that doesn't break the chain,
it just stops it from cutting into your skin unnoticed.

If you resent children or dependents for being your
reason to stay…
If love feels tangled with obligation and rage…
If you hate yourself for feeling this way…
You're not heartless.
You're not harmful.
You're not a bad parent, partner, or caregiver.

You're carrying a responsibility that came with no
consent clause, and no relief valve.
And resenting the weight doesn't mean you love them
less.

It means you're tired of carrying survival alone.

Love should not be the only thing keeping you alive,
and when it is,
the resentment deserves care,
not condemnation.

You're allowed to need support for yourself,
not just be the reason someone else survives.

Chapter 22
Being Mad That Staying Alive Is Now Your Responsibility

There's a specific kind of rage no one prepares you for.
Not crisis rage.
Not despair rage.
Not the kind where everything is on fire and people
rush in with clipboards and concern.

This is administrative rage.
The rage that shows up after you survive,
when staying alive quietly becomes your job,
and no one asks if you wanted the promotion.

At First, Staying Alive Was an Event

There was a moment.
A crisis.
A turning point.
An intervention.
A decision, or a delay.

People showed up.
Systems activated.
Urgency justified everything.

You weren't responsible yet.
You were being saved.
You were allowed to fall apart.
You were allowed to be a mess.
You were allowed to need help without explaining
yourself.

It was terrifying, but it was contained.

Then the Hand-Off Happened

Quietly.
No meeting.
No warning.
No instruction manual.
One day you realized:
"Oh. I'm in charge now."

Of:
- Meds.
- Appointments.
- Coping.
- Monitoring.
- Not letting things get "that bad" again.

Survival went from emergency response to personal maintenance.

And that pissed you off.

"You're Doing Better" Is a Trap Sentence

Because "better" comes with expectations.

If you're better, you should:
- Manage it.
- Stay on top of it.
- Not scare people anymore.

Your pain is now your responsibility to contain.
Not too loud.
Not too messy.
Not too visible.
You're not allowed to fall apart the same way twice.
Once you survive, collapse becomes inconvenient.

**Maintenance Is Exhausting When You Never
Wanted the Assignment**

Every day requires decisions.
Do I take the meds?
Do I go to the appointment?
Do I tell the truth or minimize again?
Do I intervene early or wait and see?

There is no neutral option.
Every choice carries weight.
And you are tired of carrying it.

Surviving was never supposed to turn into a lifelong
subscription service,
but here you are,
renewing it daily because the cancellation policy is
unacceptable.

**People Treat Survival like a Moral Obligation
They say:**

"You have to take care of yourself."
"You owe it to yourself."
"You owe it to the people who love you."

That last one lands like a threat.

Because now staying alive isn't just about you.
It's about not disappointing anyone.
Not hurting anyone.
Not undoing the effort they put in.

Survival becomes a duty.
Not a desire.

You Miss When Someone Else Was Watching the Edge

Here's the quiet truth no one admits:
You miss when someone else was responsible for noticing.
When professionals checked in.
When people asked real questions.
When you didn't have to self-report your own risk level.

Now the edge is yours to monitor.
And some days that feels like too much power for someone who's already exhausted.

Resentment Builds when there's No Opt-Out Clause

There is no vacation from this.
No pause button.
No "I'm done for today."

You don't get to say:
"I maintained myself long enough. Someone else take over."

So resentment creeps in, not because you want to die, but because you're sick of managing not dying.

You resent that:
- Your reward for surviving is more work.
- The bar never lowers.
- Staying alive isn't neutral, it's labor.

Daily.
Relentless.
Unpaid.

People Confuse This Anger with Ingratitude

They say:
"But you're alive."
"Isn't that what matters?"

As if existence is payment enough.
As if the cost doesn't count once the outcome is
acceptable.

You're not ungrateful.
You're exhausted by the ongoing labor of survival.

This Anger Doesn't Mean You Want to Give Up

Let's be clear.
Being mad about the responsibility of staying alive is
not the same as wanting to stop living.

It's wanting relief from the maintenance burden.
It's wanting someone to acknowledge that survival
didn't end the work, it created it.

Sometimes you're mad that you lived.
Not because you want to die, but because continuing
feels like a weight you didn't consent to carry forever.

That doesn't make you wrong.
It makes you honest.

You're allowed to Say This Feels like Too Much

You're allowed to think:
- "I didn't ask for this level of responsibility."
- "I didn't choose this role."
- "I'm doing it anyway, and I hate that I have to."

Those thoughts are not a failure.
They are a cost assessment.

I'm not going to reframe this as empowerment.
I'm not going to call it a gift.
I'm not going to pretend responsibility feels noble.
Sometimes it feels like a weight you wake up already holding.

And still, you carry it.

Not cheerfully.
Not bravely.
Not because you're inspired.
But because you're already here, and leaving would cause more damage than staying.

That's not hope.
That's obligation mixed with stubbornness.

If you're mad that staying alive is now your responsibility…
If survival feels like maintenance you never consented to…
If continuing feels like work instead of hope…
You're not failing.
You're not ungrateful.
You're not secretly wanting to disappear.

You're acknowledging that survival has an ongoing
cost, and you're the one paying it.

Sometimes staying alive isn't about wanting to.
It's about shouldering the responsibility anyway,
even while resenting the hell out of it.

And yeah.
You're allowed to be angry about that
and keep going anyway.

That's not optimism.
That's survival with the volume turned all the way up
on the truth.

Chapter 23
Staying Alive Out of Spite

I didn't stay alive because I found peace.
I stayed alive because fuck you, that's why.

Not you, you.

The pain.
The bullshit.
The voice that said, "This is all there is."

Spite is an underrated fuel source.

Hope Is Optional. Stubbornness Is Not.

Hope is fragile.
Hope needs tending.
Hope asks you to believe things will get better
and honestly, that's a big ask when your brain has a
documented history of lighting itself on fire.

Spite, on the other hand?
Spite is sturdy.
Spite doesn't need optimism.
Spite doesn't care about outcomes.
Spite just says, "Absolutely fucking not."

People love survival stories powered by hope.
I didn't have that kind.

I had:
- Curiosity that wouldn't shut up.
- A refusal to let pain win by default.
- A petty, feral instinct that said, "Nope."

Some days I stayed alive because I wanted things to
improve.
Other days I stayed alive because I wanted to see what
happened next.
And some days?
I stayed alive because quitting felt like letting
something win.

Pain Wanted the Last Word

Pain is arrogant.
It tells you it's permanent.
It tells you it knows how your story ends.
It tells you there's nothing left worth staying for.

Spite looks at that and says:
"Bold claim. Prove it."

Spite doesn't need a plan.
It doesn't need belief.
It just needs a pulse and a middle finger.

There were days I didn't stay alive because I wanted to
live.
I stayed alive because dying felt like agreeing with
every voice that ever told me I was too much,
too broken,
too difficult to keep.

Fuck that.

Curiosity Is a Lifeline Nobody Talks About

Here's something deeply unromantic but wildly
effective:
Curiosity.

Not big, meaningful curiosity.
Small, dumb curiosity.

Like:

- What happens tomorrow?
- What if something weird happens?
- What if I miss something unexpectedly good?
- What if I outlive this feeling just to be annoying?

Curiosity keeps the door cracked when everything else slams shut.

You don't need to want to live forever.
You just need to wonder what happens next.

Spite Is a Boundary

Staying alive out of spite is setting a boundary with despair.

It's saying:
"You don't get to decide for me."

It's refusing to let pain rewrite your entire existence as a cautionary tale.

It's saying:
"You hurt me, but you don't own me."

That's not inspirational.
That's territorial.

Some Days, Survival Is a Protest

Some days staying alive feels like resistance.

Not graceful resistance.
Not noble resistance.

Messy.
Teeth-gritted.
"I'm not done yet" resistance.

You don't stay because life is beautiful.
You stay because you refuse to let the worst moments
of your life be the final edit.

Sometimes survival is crawling through the day
thinking:
"I will not give this the satisfaction."

Spite Doesn't Mean You're Okay

Let's be clear.
Staying alive out of spite does not mean:
- You're healed.
- You're stable.
- You've made peace with anything.

It means you're still here.

That's it.

And sometimes, that's enough.

Spite keeps you eating something when you don't care.
Spite gets you out of bed just to prove you can.
Spite keeps you breathing because you're not about to
disappear quietly.

Is it healthy?
Debatable.

Is it effective?
Absolutely.

People Don't Like This Kind of Survival

This kind of staying makes people uncomfortable.

They want:
- Gratitude
- Meaning
- Lessons learned

They don't want:
- Pettiness
- Rage
- "I lived because I refused to die quietly."

But survival doesn't owe anyone a moral narrative.
You don't have to want life to stay alive.
You don't have to feel grateful.
You don't have to see the point.
You just have to stay.

There Is No Higher Purpose Required

You don't need:
- A calling.
- A destiny.
- A reason that sounds good in therapy.

You don't owe the universe productivity, inspiration, or redemption.

Staying alive is not a contract.
It's a choice.

Repeated.
Imperfect.
Sometimes angry.

Some Days, Spite Is the Only Thing That Shows Up

On the days when:
- Hope is gone.
- Coping skills are useless.
- Everything feels heavy and pointless.

Spite steps in and says:
"Fine. We'll stay anyway."
Not forever.
Not gracefully.
Just today.

Defiance

There is no peaceful ending here.
With the quiet, stubborn refusal to let pain be the author
of your ending.

You don't stay alive because life is good.
You stay alive because you are not finished
contradicting the lie that this is all there is.

Sometimes the most honest reason you're still here is
the simplest one…
You refused to be erased.

And if that's what kept you breathing?

Good.
Spite counts.

Chapter 24
When Coping Skills Stop Working

At some point, the tools betray you.
Not loudly.
Not dramatically.
Not with a warning label.
They just…stop doing their job.

The breathing doesn't slow your heart anymore.
The grounding exercises feel like bullshit you're
reciting to a body that has already decided to panic.
The journaling turns into word vomit with no relief.
The mantras sound hollow.
The routines feel like chores instead of lifelines.

You light the candle.
You take the walk.
You name five things you can see.
Your nervous system looks at your carefully curated
coping toolbox and says,
"Cute. Still not okay."

And that's when the panic changes shape.
Not the heart-racing, doom spiral kind.
The quieter one.
"What happens when even my survival tricks stop
working?"

The Lie: "You Have the Tools Now"

People love to say this like it's a guarantee.
You went to therapy.
You learned the skills.
You practiced.
You did the worksheets.

So you should be fine now.

Except coping skills are not armor.
They're umbrellas.
They work until the storm decides to get personal.
And when the rain turns sideways, the wind rips the
umbrella inside out, and everything floods anyway,
everyone looks at you like,
"Well… did you try holding it better?"

Coping skills are sold like permanent upgrades.
Like once you unlock them, distress has a ceiling.
Like pain respects preparation.

That is a fucking lie.

Skills Fail When the Load Exceeds Capacity

Here's the unsexy truth no one puts on a handout:
Coping skills don't fail because you're bad at them.

They fail because:
- The stress stacked too high.
- The grief compounded.
- The trauma layers started talking to each other.
- The burnout finally caught up.

Skills assume a baseline of capacity.
When that baseline is gone, you're not coping.
You're enduring.

And no worksheet prepares you for that.
Sometimes life just looks at your progress and says,
"Cool story. Here's more than you can hold."

The Special Hell of Knowing Better and Still Struggling

This is the part that fucks with your head the most.
You know what to do.
You can explain it.
Teach it.
Recite it like scripture.

And yet here you are,
still spiraling,
still drowning,
still barely holding on.

So shame jumps in immediately:
"Why isn't this working?"
"What's wrong with me?"
"I should be better at this by now."

Congratulations.
You're struggling and self-flagellating.
Gold star.

Knowing the map does not make the terrain easier.
Sometimes it just makes you angrier that you're still
lost.

Coping Skills Are Built for Maintenance, Not Collapse

Let's be clear:
Most coping skills are designed for:
- Daily stress.
- Mild dysregulation.
- Preventative care.

They are not designed for:
- Active trauma.
- Compounding losses.
- Long-term depletion.
- Existential exhaustion

Trying to breathe through systemic collapse is like trying to put out a house fire with a squirt gun.

You're not weak.
You're outmatched.

When the Tools Fail, Your Brain Gets Mean

When nothing works, your brain doesn't get compassionate.
It gets cruel.

It says:
- "See? You're hopeless."
- "This is why nothing ever changes."
- "Everyone else can handle this."
- "You should be better than this."

So now you're not just overwhelmed.
You're overwhelmed and blaming yourself for being overwhelmed.

Which is wildly inefficient.
And deeply familiar.

Improvising Survival Is Not Healing, It's Triage

When coping skills stop working, you don't gracefully pivot into growth.
You improvise.

You white-knuckle.
You numb out.
You isolate.
You dissociate more than you'd like.
You do things you thought you were "past."
You survive however you can.

Sometimes that looks messy.
Sometimes it looks unproductive.
Sometimes it looks like bare minimum functioning and
calling that a win because the alternative is not an
option.

That's not regression.
That's triage.
And triage is ugly by design.

This Is Where People Panic About You

When your usual tools stop working, people notice.
You're not bouncing back.
You're not reassuring them.
You're not performing recovery correctly.

So they panic.
They suggest more tools.
More strategies.
More effort.

As if you haven't already thrown the entire coping-
skills drawer at the problem.
As if trying harder magically creates capacity.

There Is No Backup Plan for When Everything Fails

Here's the part nobody wants to say out loud:
Sometimes there is no next step.
No technique.
No hack.
No silver bullet.

Sometimes all you have is:
- Staying alive.
- Getting through the hour.
- Not making it worse.

And that has to count.
Even though it feels pathetic.
Even though it feels like failure.

This Is Not the Part Where I Tell You to Keep Trying

I'm not going to say "don't give up."
I'm not going to say "this too shall pass."

Sometimes things don't pass quickly.
Sometimes they camp out and refuse to leave.
Sometimes the most compassionate thing you can do is
stop demanding performance from a system that is
already collapsing.

If your coping skills stopped working…
If the tools you relied on suddenly feel useless…
If you're improvising survival again and wondering
what the hell happened…
You didn't fail.

Your nervous system is overloaded.

Your capacity is depleted.
Your pain exceeded the plan.

That doesn't mean you're broken beyond repair.
It means you're human in a moment that requires more
than coping.

Sometimes survival isn't pretty.
Sometimes it isn't skilled.
Sometimes it's just staying.

And if all you're doing right now is getting through
without disappearing…
That's not weakness.
That's the raw, unglamorous truth of what happens
when the tools fail and you keep breathing anyway.

Chapter 25
Dark Humor Kept Me Alive

If laughing at my own suffering is wrong, then arrest me.

I'll be in the corner making jokes about my mugshot.

Dark humor didn't show up because I was avoiding pain.
It showed up because pain was already there, unpacked, overstaying its welcome, and eating my groceries.

Dark humor is not denial.

It's what happens when your brain is on fire and you decide to roast marshmallows over it instead of letting the whole thing burn you down.

I don't joke because I'm not hurting.
I joke because I am.

Jokes Are Not Denial; they're Translation.

People love to say,
"You're using humor to avoid your feelings."

No.

I'm using humor to get near them without drowning.

Some feelings are too big to approach head-on.
They don't respond to earnestness.
They don't care about insight.

They need a side door.
A punchline.
A joke sharp enough to cut a hole in the wall so the truth can breathe.

Laughter isn't me pretending things don't hurt.
It's me saying, "They hurt so much I need a crowbar to get close."
A joke says, "This is killing me," without making everyone panic.
A laugh says," I'm still here," without promising I'm okay.

Dark Humor Is Control in a World That Took It

Trauma steals your agency.
It decides what your body does.
What your brain fixates on.
What memories show up uninvited.

Dark humor gives a sliver of control back.

When I joke about my pain, I decide the framing.
I choose the words.
I hold the mic.
I'm not being dissected.
I'm narrating.

That's not avoidance.
That's reclamation.

People Hate It Because It Makes Them Uncomfortable

Let's be honest.

Dark humor doesn't bother people because it's
unhealthy.
It bothers them because it refuses to sanitize reality.

They want pain to be:
- Quiet
- Palatable
- Inspirational

Dark humor says:
"Actually, this is fucked up, and I'm still breathing.
Laugh with me or look away."

And a lot of people would rather look away.

Laughter Is a Pressure Valve

Humor doesn't fix anything.
It doesn't make trauma noble.
It doesn't make grief poetic.
It releases pressure.

You laugh so you don't scream.
You joke so you don't disappear.
You find something absurd because the alternative is
going under.

That's not denial.
That's physics.

You Can Joke and Still Be Serious

This one fries people's brains.
They think if you can joke about it, it must not be that
bad.

Wrong.

Sometimes the darker the joke, the closer it is to the truth.

I joke about the things that almost took me out.
Because if I don't laugh, they get too loud.

The humor isn't proof of resilience.
It's evidence of proximity.

Dark Humor Is Community

There's a specific kind of laughter that only happens between people who've been there.
It's not light.
It's not bubbly.
It's recognition.
"Oh. You too."

No explanation.
No backstory.
Just a shared understanding that some things are too real to dress up nicely.

That kind of laughter doesn't minimize pain.
It lets you stand next to it without collapsing.

"You Shouldn't Joke About That" Is a Privilege Statement

People who say this usually haven't needed humor to survive.
They think jokes are optional.
A personality trait.
A vibe.

For some of us, humor wasn't a preference.
It was the difference between staying or not.

When you've been that close to the edge, you stop
caring if your survival tools make people
uncomfortable.

You care if they work.

Humor Doesn't Mean I'm Okay

Let's be painfully clear:
If I'm joking, it does not mean I'm fine.
If I'm laughing, it does not mean I'm healed.
If I'm being funny, it does not mean I'm minimizing
my pain.

It means I'm still here.
That's it.

Sometimes the Joke Is All That's Left

There were moments when the joke was the only thing
standing between me and the void.
Not hope.
Not plans.
Not belief in a better future.
Just the ability to say something fucked up and laugh at
it long enough to stay.

That laugh didn't cure anything.
It bought time.
And sometimes time is the difference between living
and not.

This Is Not a Comedy Special

I'm not romanticizing this.
Dark humor doesn't make pain cute.
It doesn't make trauma inspiring.
It doesn't solve anything.
It just keeps some of us breathing.

And if that offends people who prefer tidy healing
narratives?

That's their problem.

If humor is how you survive…
If jokes are how you tell the truth without breaking…
If laughter is the rope you grab when everything else
slips…
You're not minimizing your pain.
You're managing it.

This doesn't end with advice or moderation.
It doesn't pivot to "healthier coping."
It doesn't ask you to soften anything.

It ends with honesty:
Dark humor didn't make my life easier.
It made it possible.
Sometimes the thing that keeps you alive looks
inappropriate, uncomfortable, and deeply
misunderstood.

And if it works?
That's enough.

Part V:
The Systems That Were Supposed To Fix It

Chapter 26
Therapy Is Not a Personality Upgrade

Let's clear something up before we go any further:
Therapy does not turn you into a calm, healed,
emotionally regulated woodland creature who drinks
water, stretches, and says things like "I'm honoring my
capacity today."

If that's what you were promised, someone sold you a
candle and called it mental health.

Therapy does not fix you.
It does not erase trauma.
It does not uninstall your brain like a bad app update.

Sometimes it just hands you a flashlight and says,
"Hey. Look at this."
Which is honestly rude.

Therapy Does Not Feel Good

Anyone who says therapy feels "healing" is cherry-
picking or lying for Instagram.

Therapy feels like:
- Crying in a chair while making deeply
  uncomfortable eye contact.
- Realizing something awful about your
  childhood on a random Tuesday at 3:07pm.
- Paying a professional to say something you
  absolutely did not want confirmed.

- Leaving emotionally flayed and then having to
  decide what to make for dinner like nothing
  happened.

You don't leave therapy glowing.
You leave therapy dissociated, overthinking, and
suddenly aware that half your personality is a trauma
response wearing a trench coat.

Congrats.

Growth.

Insight Is Not Relief (And That Feels Like a Scam)

Here's the cruel bait-and-switch:
Understanding why you're like this does not magically
make you stop being like this.

You can know:
- Where your anxiety came from.
- Why you people-please.
- Why conflict shuts you down.
- Why joy feels suspicious.

And still feel all of it in your body like your nervous
system never got the memo.

Because trauma does not live in logic.

So while your therapist is calmly saying,
"And how did that make you feel?"
Your nervous system is screaming,
"Cool story. Still dying."

Self-awareness is not the same as relief.

Sometimes it's just pain with better vocabulary.

When Your Therapist Says Something True and You Want to Throw a Chair

This is a sacred therapy moment.

Your therapist says something soft.
Careful.
Clinically gentle.
And absolutely fucking lethal.

Something like:
- "I think part of you is afraid of what happens if you stop surviving."
- "You might be holding onto this pain because it's familiar."
- "What if you didn't push yourself this hard?"
- "Do you think XYZ is happening because of ABC?"

And immediately
IMMEDIATELY
your soul leaves your body,
circles the room once,
and comes back holding a chair.

Internally, you say:
Fuck you.
Respectfully.
With love.

Outwardly, you nod.
You blink slowly.
You say, "Yeah… that makes sense."

You do not say:
"I hate that sentence and I will be thinking about it at
3:12 a.m. for the rest of my life."

You do not say:
"How dare you notice that."

You flip them off energetically.
It's a very polite middle finger.
A therapeutic middle finger.
One with boundaries.
One your therapist (at least mine) loves.
Because here's the thing:
you're not mad because they're wrong.
You're mad because they're right,
and right now that truth is wildly inconvenient.

That coping mechanism?
The one they just gently suggested you examine?
That's not a bad habit.
That's load-bearing trauma architecture.
That's the *Jenga* piece holding the whole fucked-up
tower upright.

You cannot just "explore what happens if you let go."
Ma'am. Sir. Licensed professional.
If I let go, this entire personality collapses like a folding
chair at a backyard barbecue.

So you nod.
You agree.
You say, "I'll think about that."

And then you go home and do exactly what you were
doing before, but now with the added spice of self-
awareness.

This is not resistance.
This is knowing that yes, the wound needs air, but also,
maybe not during rush hour.

This is saying:
I hear you.
I believe you.
I am simply not ready to detonate my only functional
survival system on a Wednesday.

And the worst part?
They know.
They see it in your eyes.
That mix of rage,
recognition,
and quiet terror.

They don't push.
They don't argue.
They just sit there like, "Yeah. Okay. We'll come back
to that when you're less feral."

So you flip them off again.
With love.
With gratitude.
With the unspoken promise that one day,
not today,
you'll deal with it.

And then you leave therapy,
get in your car, and think:
"Goddammit. They're so annoying."
Which, translated, means:
"They saw me."
And that is somehow worse.

Therapy Can Make You Harder to Be Around

No one warns you about this.

Once you've been in therapy for a while, you get:
- Language
- Boundaries
- Awareness
- The audacity

You stop tolerating shit you used to swallow.
You name patterns.
You ask for clarity.
You don't laugh things off as easily.
And people hate that.

They liked you better when you were quieter.
More accommodating.
Less aware of your own limits.

Therapy doesn't always make your life better.
Sometimes it just makes it more honest.
And honesty can be lonely as hell.

Your Therapist Is Not a Wizard

Let's kill another myth while we're here:
Your therapist does not have the answers.
They are not a guru.
They are not a mind reader.
They are not handing you enlightenment on a clipboard.

Sometimes they miss things.
Sometimes they misunderstand you.
Sometimes you outgrow them.

Sometimes you sit in silence staring at the carpet
because you don't know how to tell the truth yet.

Therapy is two humans in a room guessing carefully.
Anyone who pretends otherwise is selling certainty they
do not possess.

You Don't Graduate From Therapy

People ask,
"Are you still in therapy?"
Like it's a rehab stint.
Like one day you just wake up healed, turn in your
badge, and ride into emotional stability.

Some people go for years.
Some go forever.
Some take breaks and come back.
Some never find a therapist who actually gets them.

None of that means you failed.
It means your brain is complicated and life keeps
happening.

Therapy Does Not Stop the Bad Thoughts

Let's be painfully clear:
Therapy does not erase suicidal ideation.
It does not delete intrusive thoughts.
It does not guarantee stability.
Sometimes it just gives you language for the chaos.

Which helps.

And also doesn't.

You can be deeply self-aware and still want to disappear sometimes.
Those are not opposites.

"Doing the Work" Becomes a Weapon

This is where therapy gets weaponized.

People hear you're in therapy and assume:
- You'll be calmer.
- You'll be easier.
- You'll stop struggling.
- You'll heal on a schedule that makes them comfortable.

And when you don't?
When you still spiral?
Still fuck up?
Still have bad days?

They get impatient.

Because apparently self-awareness was supposed to cure you.

It doesn't.

Sometimes Therapy Just Keeps You Alive

This is the part no one romanticizes.
Sometimes therapy doesn't make you happy.
It doesn't make you better.
It doesn't make life easier.
Sometimes it just keeps you here.

It gives your pain a witness.

It gives you a pause between thought and action.
It gives you somewhere to say the unspeakable without
being punished for it.

That's not a glow-up.
That's maintenance.

No Transformation. Just Reality.

I'm not here to tell you therapy saved me.
It didn't.

Sometimes it helps.
Sometimes it pisses me off.
Sometimes it cracks something open I wasn't ready to
see.
Sometimes all it does is make the unbearable slightly
more survivable.

And sometimes that has to be enough.

If you're in therapy and still struggling, you're not
doing it wrong.
You're not resistant.
You're not broken.
You're living with shit that does not resolve cleanly.

Therapy is not a cure.
It's not a personality upgrade.
It's not a guarantee.

It's a tool.
A space.
A witness.

And sometimes the most honest outcome is this:
You're still you.

Still messy.
Still fighting.
Still not fixed.

Therapy doesn't make life easy.
It just makes you slightly more conscious while you
keep going anyway.

And yeah, sometimes that consciousness makes you
want to tell your therapist to fuck off.

Lovingly.

Because they saw you too clearly.
And you're not ready to let that go yet.

Chapter 27
Medication: Not a Miracle, Not a Moral Failure

Let's start with the thing everyone tiptoes around like it
might explode:

Medication is not cheating.
It is also not magic.
It is a roulette wheel you spin with a prescription pad
and a prayer.

Some people treat meds like a miracle cure.
Others treat them like a personal weakness.

There is apparently no middle ground,
just judgment,
opinions,
and unsolicited *TED Talks* from people whose brains
have never tried to eat them alive.

If you take meds, you're either "finally doing better" or
"not trying hard enough."
If you don't, you're either "so strong" or "in denial."
There is no neutral setting.
Only commentary.

So let's be clear:
Medication will not save you.
Medication will not ruin you.
Medication will not turn you into a different person.

It is not enlightenment in pill form.
It is not a personality transplant.
It is chemistry attempting to negotiate a ceasefire.

The Audacity of Trial and Error

Here's how it usually goes:
You're miserable.
Someone suggests meds.
You resist because you're strong,
scared,
stubborn,
tired of being disappointed,
or all four.

Eventually, desperation wins.

You take the pill.

Nothing happens.
Or everything happens.

Side effects arrive like an uninvited houseguest who
refuses to leave:
- Nausea.
- Brain fog.
- Insomnia.
- Night sweats.
- Emotional flat-lining.
- Libido packed its bags and left town.

You wait the mandatory six to eight weeks like a good
patient, wondering if this is working or if you're just
tired in a new font.

Sometimes it helps.
Sometimes it absolutely does not.
Sometimes it helps a little,
which somehow feels worse than not helping at all.

Too much and you're numb.
Too little and your thoughts go feral again.
Wrong one and suddenly you can't sleep,
can't eat,
can't feel,
or can't stop sweating like you're being interrogated
under hot lights.

There is nothing glamorous about this.

Medication Is Not a Fix, It's Scaffolding

Medication does not fix your trauma.
It does not teach coping skills.
It does not give you motivation.
It does not erase intrusive thoughts or cure existential
dread.

At best, it turns the volume down.

Not off.
Down.

Enough that you can exist without feeling like your
brain is actively trying to sabotage you every waking
second.

And even then, it's inconsistent.

Some days it helps.
Some days it barely registers.
Some days you wonder if it's doing anything at all.

Which inevitably leads to someone asking,
"Do you really need it?"

Yes.
And also sometimes no.

And also it's none of your fucking business.

Medication is scaffolding.
It holds things steady enough for you to stay upright.
It does not rebuild the structure.
It just keeps it from collapsing while you're still inside
it.

The Identity Crisis Nobody Warned You About

Medication doesn't just affect symptoms.
It messes with your sense of self.

You start asking:
- Is this me or the meds?
- Am I calmer or just numb?
- Is this relief or am I losing something?
- Who was I without this?

People say,
"Wouldn't you rather feel better?"
As if "better" is a simple concept.
As if your brain hasn't already complicated that beyond
recognition.

Sometimes medication gives you access to parts of
yourself that were buried under constant survival mode.

Sometimes it changes the flavor of your suffering,
not the fact of it.

Both can be true.

The Shame Layer (Because There's Always a Shame Layer)

Let's talk about the internalized bullshit.

The voice that whispers:
- "If I were stronger, I wouldn't need this."
- "Other people cope without pills."
- "I should be able to do this on my own."
- "I'm taking the easy way out."

That voice is lying.

Needing medication is not a failure of willpower.
It is not proof you didn't do therapy "right."
It is not evidence that you're broken beyond repair.
It means your brain needed backup.

People don't shame diabetics for insulin.
They don't tell asthmatics to breathe better.
But brains?
Brains are apparently expected to raw-dog chemistry
and call it growth.

Suffering is not proof of effort.

Medication Doesn't Fix the World You're Living In

Here's an inconvenient truth:
You can be medicated and still miserable.

Because medication does not:
- Remove trauma.
- Fix capitalism.
- Heal abusive relationships.

- Make the world gentler.
- Teach people how to treat you better.

You can be medicated and still overwhelmed.
You can be medicated and still depressed.
You can be medicated and still want to disappear
sometimes.

That does not mean the meds failed.
It means life is still happening.

The Pressure to Be "Better" Now

Once you're on medication, expectations show up fast.
People want results.
Immediate ones.
They want you calmer.
Happier.
More functional.
Less inconvenient.
And if you're not?
They assume something's wrong.

With you.

Not the dosage.
Not the medication.
Not the unrealistic timeline.

You.

Stopping Medication Is Not Redemption

Let's flip the script.
Coming off medication is not always a triumph.
Sometimes it's necessary.

Sometimes it's hell.
Sometimes it's both.
Withdrawal can be brutal.
Emotions come back loud.
Your brain reboots without warning.
And if you decide to stay on meds long-term?
You'll meet people who act like that's tragic.
As if stability is something you're supposed to outgrow.

There Is No Ethical High Ground Here

Taking medication does not make you weak.
Not taking medication does not make you strong.
There is no moral hierarchy.

There is just:
- What helps.
- What harms.
- What you can tolerate.
- What keeps you alive.

That's it.

Medication is not a miracle.
But it's also not a moral failure.

It's a tool.
An option.
A gamble.

Sometimes it helps.
Sometimes it doesn't.
Sometimes it makes things survivable.
Sometimes it just changes the texture of the struggle.

That's not inspiring.

It's realistic.

If you take medication and still struggle, you're not
failing.
If you don't take medication and still struggle, you're
not refusing help.
If you tried medication and it didn't work, you're not
hopeless.

Medication is not a cure.
It is not a personality flaw.
It is not a character defect.
It's one more way humans try to stay alive in brains
that didn't come with instructions.

Staying alive sometimes means choosing the least worst
option and learning to live with the ambiguity.

Chapter 28
Diagnoses: The Labels, the Lies, and the Lifetime Subscription

At some point, your mental health file starts to look less like a chart and more like a ransom note written by multiple clinicians who never talked to each other.

Anxiety.
Depression.
PTSD.
ADHD.
Maybe bipolar.
Maybe borderline.
Maybe "unspecified mood disorder" because someone needed to wrap this appointment up before lunch.

It starts to feel like a fucked-up Pokémon collection.
Not because you want them.
Because something is wrong, and nobody can agree on what flavor.

You don't collect diagnoses for fun.
You collect them because you're bleeding internally and everyone keeps arguing over which label the blood belongs to.

The First Diagnosis: Relief with a Side of False Hope

The first diagnosis feels like oxygen.
"Oh thank God, I'm not lazy."
"Oh thank God, there's a name for this."
"Oh thank God, I'm not just bad at being human."

You think:
Now we can fix it.

Adorable.

The first diagnosis is hope wrapped in clinical
language.
It makes you believe this is a puzzle with an edge piece.
That if you just follow the treatment plan, you'll unlock
the "before and after" version of yourself.

Spoiler: that version does not exist.

Anxiety Disorders: The Overachieving Alarm System

Anxiety is usually the first label slapped on because
it's...
Polite.
Non-threatening.
Palatable.

You're anxious.
Not traumatized.
Not terrified.
Not living in a body that learned hypervigilance was the
price of survival.

Anxiety gets described like a personality quirk.

Nervous.
Type A.
High-strung.

No one tells you it feels like living in a body that treats
neutral stimuli as life-or-death threats.
Anxiety is not "worrying too much."

It's:

- Your heart launching into orbit over emails.
- Your body preparing for violence in grocery stores.
- Your nervous system assuming danger is imminent and personal.

And when treatment doesn't "work," you're told:
Try harder.
Meditate more.
Breathe correctly.

Meanwhile your body is screaming,
"WE ARE NOT SAFE AND I DO NOT CARE
ABOUT YOUR AFFIRMATIONS."

Depression: The Diagnosis That Blames You for Being Tired of Carrying Everything

Depression shows up once anxiety stops being cute.
When you're not just panicking, you're exhausted.
When survival starts feeling like manual labor with no pay and no days off.

Depression gets described as sadness.
Which is insulting.
Depression is not sadness.

It's:

- Gravity.
- Cognitive fog.
- Emotional deadness that makes joy feel like a rumor.
- The quiet knowledge that everything requires more effort than you have.

And the worst part?
Depression makes wanting help feel impossible.

You don't just feel bad, you feel pointless.
And then you're judged for not advocating for yourself
loudly enough.

PTSD & Complex Trauma: When Your Past Refuses to Stay in the Past

PTSD is where things get uncomfortable.
Because now we're not talking about mood.
We're talking about memory.
Body memory.
Nervous system wiring that learned lessons you cannot
unlearn with insight alone.

Trauma doesn't show up as flashbacks all the time.

It shows up as:
- Overreacting to small things.
- Underreacting to big things.
- Dissociating mid-conversation.
- Feeling unsafe in situations that "should" be fine.

Complex trauma is especially cruel because it rarely
comes with a single event.

No headline.
No courtroom.
No clear villain.

Just years of:
- Inconsistency.
- Emotional neglect.
- Fear without language.

And then people ask,
"Why are you like this?"
You don't know.

Your body does.

ADHD: The Diagnosis That Explains Everything and Fixes Almost Nothing

ADHD diagnosis is a revelation.

Suddenly:
- You're not lazy.
- You're not careless.
- You're not irresponsible.

You're neurologically incompatible with linear expectations.
And also?
It explains absolutely everything and fixes almost nothing.

Because now you know why you struggle, but you still have to live in a world designed to punish your brain specifically.

ADHD meds help.
Sometimes.

Other times they just make you a focused version of overwhelmed.

And if you're late-diagnosed?
You get the bonus grief package:
All the shame for things that were never your fault.
All the punishment for traits you didn't choose.
All the coping mechanisms that look like moral failures
in hindsight.

**Bipolar, Mood Disorders, and the "Are You Sure?"
Phase**

This is where clinicians start disagreeing.
Is it bipolar?
Is it trauma?
Is it emotional dysregulation?
Is it just stress?

You become a case study.
You start tracking yourself obsessively.
Mood charts.
Sleep logs.
Symptom timelines.
You stop asking how you feel and start asking how you
present.

And every med trial becomes a roulette wheel:
"Will this help?"
"Will this flatten me?"
"Will this light me on fire emotionally?"

Side effects become their own diagnosis.

Personality Disorders: When the Label Feels Like an Accusation

Nothing hits quite like being told your personality is the problem.
Especially borderline.

Suddenly:
- Your emotions are suspect.
- Your reactions are scrutinized.
- Your pain is seen as manipulative by default.

Everything you feel gets filtered through pathology.
You're not hurt, you're splitting.
You're not angry, you're dysregulated.
You're not reacting, you're being borderline.

Which is a great way to make someone stop trusting themselves entirely.

And once that label is on your file?
Good luck getting it off.
Or being heard cleanly again.

Misdiagnosis: When Treatment Makes You Worse

Misdiagnosis is psychological gaslighting with a prescription pad.

You do everything right.
You take the meds.
You show up to therapy.
You try.
And nothing improves.

So you assume the problem is you.

Not the diagnosis.
Not the system.
Not the mismatch.
You internalize failure for symptoms that were never
addressed properly.

Underdiagnosis: When Functioning Becomes a Weapon against You

High-functioning is the most invalidating compliment
in mental health.

It means:
You can suffer quietly enough to be ignored.
You only get help once you break publicly.

Until then?
You're fine.
You're coping.
You're resilient.

Which translates to:
You're on your own.

The Diagnosis Becomes the Lens

Eventually, the label stops being information.
It becomes identity, whether you want it or not.

People talk to you differently.
Doctors listen differently.
You listen to yourself differently.
You start narrating your life like a chart note.
Self-awareness turns into self-surveillance.
And you lose the ability to just be a person having a
hard day.

Permanent Diagnoses: The Grief No One Prepares You For

Some diagnoses don't resolve.
There is no finish line.
No cure.
No final form.
You don't get better.
You get managed.
And that realization hurts in a specific, quiet way.

You grieve:
- The life without constant maintenance.
- The fantasy of "one day."
- The ease other people take for granted.

And no one throws a funeral for that loss.

Diagnoses are not answers.
They're translations.
Imperfect ones.

They don't save you.
They don't doom you.
They don't explain everything.
They just give shape to chaos that was already there.

You are not your diagnoses.
But they are part of your reality now.
And pretending they're temporary nearly killed you.

You are living in a body and brain that finally has a
name,
still figuring out what the hell to do with that
information,
and continuing anyway.

Which is not inspirational.

It's just real.

And exhausting.

And, unfortunately…

Still yours.

Chapter 29
When Your Body Is the Problem and the Evidence

The crime scene is me.

There's a special kind of hell that comes with realizing your body is both the problem and the proof.

I don't have to explain what's wrong.
I'm standing in it.
The evidence is visible.
Audible.
Measurable.

Heart rate.
Weight.
Scars.
Fatigue.
Flinching.
Pain that doesn't behave.

My body is not a witness.
It's the crime scene that keeps getting reopened.

You Can't Gaslight a Symptom That Won't Shut Up

People love to tell you it's "in your head."
Cool.
My head is attached to my body, which is currently malfunctioning like a haunted appliance.

When your body reacts before your thoughts do,
when your hands shake,
your stomach drops,
your chest locks up,
there is no room for denial.

Your body doesn't debate.
Your body doesn't care about context.
Your body does not accept reassurance.
It just reacts.

And now you're stuck trying to live in the same place
that keeps betraying you.

The Body Keeps the Receipts (And Will Read Them Aloud)

Your body remembers things you worked very hard to
forget.

It remembers:
- Fear
- Hunger
- Restraint
- Impact
- Neglect
- Being ignored

It remembers even when your brain edits the story to be
more socially acceptable.

You can say, "It wasn't that bad."
Your body responds with nausea,
migraines,

tension,
dissociation,
and pain that has no clear cause.

Bold of you to think you get to rewrite history.

Medical Appointments: Where You Beg to Be Believed

Nothing will humble you faster than sitting in a sterile room explaining symptoms that don't fit neatly into a chart.

You list what hurts.
They check vitals.
They nod.
They suggest stress.
They suggest weight.
They suggest mindfulness.
They suggest maybe you're just sensitive.

You leave with:
- No answers.
- New shame.
- The creeping sense that your body is misbehaving incorrectly.

Your body is screaming.
The system hears static.

When Your Body Makes You the Least Reliable Narrator

Here's the mindfuck:
You start doubting yourself.

Is this pain real?
Am I exaggerating?
Am I weak?
Am I dramatic?
Is everyone else just better at tolerating being alive?

Your body gives you data.
The world tells you it's anecdotal.

So you learn to downplay.
To push through.
To ignore warning signs.

Until your body escalates.
Because subtlety didn't work.

Existing in a Body That Can't Be Trusted

When your body is unpredictable,
safety becomes theoretical.

You plan exits.
You scan bathrooms.
You memorize where to sit,
where to lean,
where to disappear if things go sideways.

You are never fully present.
Because your body might turn on you at any moment.

Pain.
Panic.
Collapse.
Freeze.

You don't relax.

You monitor.
Your body is not your home.
It's a volatile roommate.

The Cruel Loop: Blame the Body, Punish the Body

And then, because we're excellent at self-destruction,
you turn on it.

You resent it.
You restrict it.
You ignore it.
You push it harder.
You shame it into compliance.
You treat your body like an enemy that needs
discipline.

Because listening didn't work.
Because compassion didn't fix it.
Because you're exhausted from negotiating with
something that never gives you clear terms.

So you punish the very thing that's already hurting.

Perfect system.
No notes.

When the Body Becomes Proof You're Not "Better"

People love progress narratives.
They want to hear you're healed.
Managing.
Thriving.
Past it.

Your body ruins that story.

It flinches at the wrong time.
It reacts to the wrong voice.
It panics in safe rooms.
It hurts when nothing is wrong.
Your body outs you.
No matter how articulate you become,
your body will tell the truth with zero regard for timing.

You Learn to Live Like Evidence Is Incriminating

You hide symptoms.
You minimize pain.
You apologize for existing loudly.
Because when your body is the proof, being seen feels
risky.

Someone might:
- Doubt you.
- Pathologize you.
- Pity you.
- Fix you wrong.
- Make it your fault.

So you disappear inside yourself.
Again.

Peace with Your Body Is Not the Assignment

I'm not going to tell you to love your body.
I'm not going to say it's trying its best.
I'm not going to give you a gratitude exercise.

Sometimes your body is a nightmare you have to
inhabit anyway.

Sometimes it hurts.

Sometimes it panics.
Sometimes it fails you publicly.
Sometimes it keeps you alive in ways that are ugly and
inconvenient.
Both can be true.

If your body feels like the problem and the evidence…
If it exposes what you'd rather keep quiet…
If it reacts before you can consent…
You're not imagining it.
You're not broken.
You're not weak.
You're living in a system that adapted to survive
something real, and now refuses to forget.

Your body is not lying.
It's telling a story no one taught it how to stop telling.

And no, there's no resolution here.
No neat reconciliation.
No moment where the body suddenly becomes safe and
compliant.

Just this:
You live inside the evidence.
You carry it everywhere.
And you keep going anyway.

Which is not inspirational.
It's just what happens when survival leaves marks and
the body refuses to pretend otherwise.

Chapter 30
The Trauma of Being Believed Too Late

They believe you now.

Congratulations.

The damage is already done.

There is a very specific kind of rage that arrives when
someone finally says,
"I believe you."

Not during the emergency.
Not when you were begging.
Not when your body was screaming loud enough to
scare people.

Now.

After the bruises faded.
After the symptoms calcified.
After your nervous system rewired itself like a haunted
house attraction that never shuts down.

They believe you now.
Which is adorable.
And useless.

Being believed too late doesn't feel like validation.
It feels like someone showing up to a house fire with a
glass of water and a thumbs-up.

The Timing Is the Violence

People act like belief is binary.
Either you have it or you don't.

That's bullshit.

Timing matters.

Belief after the damage isn't repair.
It's commentary.
It's someone standing over the wreckage going,
"Wow. Yeah. That was bad."

Cool.

Where the fuck were you when it mattered?

When belief arrives late, it doesn't soothe.
It scrapes.

Because now you're left holding two realities at once:
    1. You were right the whole time.
    2. It cost you everything to prove it.

"I Didn't Know" Is Not the Defense You Think It Is

People love to say,
"I didn't realize it was that serious."
Yeah.
Neither did I (because you kept telling me it wasn't).

You told me I was dramatic.
You told me to calm down.

You told me it would pass.
You told me to be grateful.
You told me other people had it worse.

So I swallowed it.
Internalized it.
Tried to survive quietly so I wouldn't inconvenience
you.

Now you're shocked I'm fucked up?
Miss me with that.

Not knowing doesn't absolve you when you actively
ignored the evidence.

Validation Doesn't Reverse Time

This is the part nobody wants to talk about.
Belief doesn't rewind the years.
It doesn't untrain hypervigilance.
It doesn't give you back the version of yourself that
trusted people to show up.
It doesn't erase the self-loathing that grew in the space
where support should've been.

It just shows you how unnecessary all that suffering
was.

Which is…not comforting.
It's infuriating.

You Grieve the Person You Might Have Been

Being believed late opens a brand-new grief portal.
You don't just grieve what happened.

You grieve what could've happened if someone had
listened sooner.
Who would I be if help had arrived before I broke
myself trying to function?
What would my nervous system feel like if safety
hadn't been theoretical?
How much pain was avoidable?

You don't get answers.
You get resentment.
And grief.
And the urge to scream into a pillow until it files a
noise complaint.

"I Believe You" Does Not Mean "I'm Accountable"

Here's a fun twist:
Late belief often comes with zero responsibility.

People will say they believe you while still refusing to
look at their role in your silence.
They believe you now, but they don't apologize for
before.
They believe you now, but they don't want to talk about
the harm of disbelief.
They believe you now, but they want to move on
quickly so things aren't awkward.

Belief without accountability is just emotional tourism.

They stop by.
They nod sympathetically.
They leave you with the mess.

The Apology You'll Never Get

Sometimes belief comes without an apology at all.
No "I'm sorry I didn't listen."
No "I should have done more."
No "I failed you."

Just quiet acknowledgment and an expectation that this
is closure.

It's not.
It's an unfinished sentence that rattles around in your
chest forever.
Because now you know they could have believed you.

They just didn't.

It Makes You Question Every Future Offer of Support

Once you've been believed too late, every future "I'm
here for you" comes with an internal eye-roll.
You don't trust it.
You don't lean into it.

You wait for the expiration date.

Because you've learned that belief has conditions.
That care has a delay.
That people often need you to be visibly destroyed
before they take you seriously.

So you stop asking.
You stop explaining.
You stop hoping someone will catch you in time.

Not because you're closed off...
Because you're trained.

The Anger Is Rational, Actually

Let's normalize something real quick:
You are allowed to be angry about being believed too
late.

Angry at doctors.
Angry at family.
Angry at friends.
Angry at systems that reward collapse and punish early
honesty.

That anger isn't bitterness.
It's clarity.
It's your nervous system recognizing that delayed care
is still harm.

There Is No Redemption Here

This is not about forgiveness.
It's not about gratitude for being believed eventually.
It's not about "at least now you know."

Fuck that.

Knowing you were right doesn't heal the damage
caused by being ignored.

Being believed too late doesn't feel like winning.
It feels like surviving a preventable injury and being
told you should be relieved the bleeding stopped.

You're not relieved.

You're tired.
You're angry.
You're carrying scars that didn't need to exist.

Being believed too late is its own trauma.
It teaches you that pain must escalate to be credible.
That suffering is only real once it's inconvenient
enough.
That quiet distress doesn't count.
And once you learn that lesson, it sticks.

If someone finally believes you and it doesn't bring
peace,
if it brings rage, grief, and a hollow "cool, now what?"
instead…
You're not ungrateful.
You're not cruel.
You're not stuck.
You're responding to the cost of being right in a world
that made you prove it the hard way.

And yeah.
That shit leaves a mark.

Part VI: Relationships, Shame, and Invisible Rules

Chapter 31
Shame: The Background Noise of Everything

Shame doesn't kick the door in.
It doesn't scream.
It doesn't demand attention.

Shame hums.
Low.
Constant.
Relentless.
Like tinnitus for your soul.

You don't wake up feeling shame.
You wake up already tuned to it.
It's the default channel,
the static under every other emotion,
the background noise that never shuts the fuck up even
when everything else goes quiet.

Joy comes with it.
Pride comes with it.
Rest definitely comes with it.

Shame is why every memory replays with commentary.
Why every mistake feels fatal.
Why neutral interactions get mentally re-edited into
evidence that you're bad, wrong, annoying, or
fundamentally defective.

Shame doesn't show up as one clear thought.

It's an atmosphere.

A quiet belief that:
- You're too much.
- You're not enough.
- You're doing life wrong.
- There's something fundamentally off about you.

Not because of anything specific you did.
Just because you exist the way you do.

Shame doesn't ask questions.
It delivers verdicts.

You can be proud for half a second before it clears its
throat and says, "Don't get cocky."
You can be hurt and it whispers,
"You're overreacting."
You can need help and it immediately asks,
"What's wrong with you?"

Shame doesn't care what actually happened.
It cares about keeping you small.

You Don't Remember Learning Shame, You Absorbed It

No one sat you down and said,
"You should hate yourself a little."

You learned it through tone.
Through silence.
Through disappointment.
Through praise that came with conditions.

You learned:
- Which emotions were acceptable.
- Which needs were inconvenient.

- Which parts of you should be hidden.
- When love was withdrawn.

So you adjusted.

You got quieter.
Smaller.
Easier.
And shame moved in like it paid rent.

It became the internal narrator saying
"You should've known better"
about things you were never taught.

The voice that insists you're at fault
even when you were a child,
powerless,
improvising,
doing the best you could with the nervous system you
had.

Shame learned early that visibility was dangerous.
That being seen invited judgment, correction,
punishment, or withdrawal.

So it took over quality control.

Better to hate yourself first than let someone else do it
better.

Shame is proactive like that.

Shame Isn't Accountability, It's Surveillance

Shame loves to cosplay as responsibility.
As humility.

As realism.
As self-awareness.

It says it's just keeping you grounded.
Keeping you from being embarrassing.
Keeping you from believing you deserve too much.

It lies.

Shame is not accountability.
It's self-surveillance.
It turns your inner world into a courtroom where you're
simultaneously the accused, the prosecutor, and the
judge…
and the sentence is always guilty.

You don't relax because shame is watching.
You don't celebrate because shame is waiting.
You don't fully enjoy anything because shame is
already preparing the comedown.

One mistake becomes a personality indictment.
One awkward moment becomes proof.
One bad day becomes confirmation that you're exactly
as flawed as you always suspected.

Shame does not scale appropriately.
Everything is maximum severity.

Shame Is Why Everything Feels Personal

A minor mistake feels catastrophic.
A neutral comment feels like rejection.
A boundary feels like you're asking for too much.
Because shame tells you, "This is evidence."

Evidence that you're difficult.
Evidence that you're failing.
Evidence that everyone will eventually see what you already believe about yourself.

Shame doesn't care about context.
It only cares about confirmation.

So you apologize constantly.
Sorry for talking.
Sorry for asking.
Sorry for needing.
Sorry for existing.

Not because you did anything wrong, but because shame taught you that your presence requires justification.

You learn to disappear politely.

Hyper-Awareness, Isolation, and the Cost of Self-Editing

Shame makes you hyper-aware and deeply lonely.
You monitor your tone.
Your reactions.
Your expressions.
Your needs.

You edit yourself in real time like you're trying not to get fired from being a person.

And the cost of all that self-management?
Isolation.

Because no one is actually meeting you.

They're meeting the version you think is least likely to
be rejected.

Shame thrives on comparison.
Everyone else looks more confident.
More functional.
More lovable.
Less exhausting.

You assume their flaws are quieter than yours.
You assume you're the only one doing life on expert
mode with no tutorial.

Shame isolates you, then uses the isolation as proof.

Shame Gets Louder When you're Already Hurting

Here's the sick irony:
The worse you're doing, the louder shame gets.
You're already exhausted.
Already overwhelmed.
Already barely holding it together.

And shame piles on:
- "Other people handle this."
- "You should be past this."
- "Why are you like this?"
- "Get it together."

As if cruelty is motivation.
As if you haven't tried hard enough already.

Shame doesn't want you dead.
It wants you compliant.
Apologetic.
Self-doubting.

So busy managing your flaws that you never ask who
taught you to hate yourself this efficiently.

This Is Not a Self-Compassion Pep Talk

I'm not going to tell you to silence shame.
I'm not going to tell you to replace it with affirmations.
I'm not going to tell you to love yourself harder.

Shame doesn't respond to cheerleading.
It responds to exposure.
Naming it.
Seeing it.
Calling it what it is.

Not truth.
Not discipline.
Not insight.
Conditioning.

There's no triumphant scene where shame evaporates
and the static cuts out completely.

That's not how this works.

Shame is sticky.
Persistent.
Resourceful.
It fades in and out.
Changes disguises.
Finds new ways to sound reasonable.

But sometimes, just sometimes, naming it lowers the
volume a notch.

Enough to breathe.

Enough to notice it isn't the same as truth.
Enough to realize you didn't invent this voice.
It was handed to you.

If shame feels like the background noise of your entire
existence…
If you feel wrong even when nothing's wrong…
If you can't shake the belief that you're fundamentally
defective…

You're not broken.

You're carrying a belief system built around survival,
not kindness.

And no, knowing that doesn't make shame disappear.

But it does one important thing:
It tells you the hum isn't proof.
It's just noise that's been playing for a very long time.

Shame has been lying to you quietly,
and you've been listening because you didn't know you
had a choice.

And now you do.

Even if you don't know what to do with that yet.

Chapter 32
Feeling Competitive About Suffering

This is the thought you swat away immediately.
Because it sounds ugly.
Because it sounds petty.
Because it sounds like you're turning pain into a
scoreboard.

And yet…
There it is.
Quiet.
Reflexive.
Automatic.

Someone shares their pain and your brain does math:
"Okay, but did you…"
"Yeah, but mine was worse because…"
"Sure, but you didn't have…"

And the second you notice it happening,
shame dogpiles on top like,
"Jesus Christ, what kind of person thinks like that?"

Nobody wants to admit this applies to them.

Too bad.

**You Don't Want to Win. You Just Don't Want to Be
Erased.**

Let's get this straight.
You are not trying to out-suffer anyone.
You are not hoping others hurt more.
You are not craving a trophy made of trauma.
You're trying to make sure your pain still counts.

Because when pain was ignored, minimized, dismissed, or compared away, your nervous system learned something brutal:

If it's not the worst, it won't be believed at all.

So comparison sneaks in, not as ego, but as self-defense.

If theirs counts, does mine disappear?

Scar Hierarchies Form When Validation Is Scarce

When care is limited, pain becomes currency.
Who had it worse?
Who lasted longer?
Who broke quieter?
Who almost didn't make it?

You didn't invent this system.
You learned it in rooms where:
- Attention went to the most extreme story.
- Help followed escalation.
- Credibility required receipts.

You adapted.

Because empathy wasn't abundant.
It was rationed.

You Learned That Being "Not That Bad" Meant Being Ignored

This is where it usually starts.
If you weren't hospitalized, it didn't count.
If you didn't attempt, it wasn't real.

If you functioned, you were "fine."

So your brain learned to rank pain.
Not to feel superior,
but to avoid disappearing.

Someone Else's Story can feel like a Threat

When someone shares something worse, something in
you flinches.
Not because you doubt them.
Not because you begrudge them.
Because your nervous system hears:
"See? Yours isn't enough."
And that fear is ancient.

So you inventory your damage.
Your timelines.
Your worst moments.
Your proof.

Not out loud.
Not proudly.

Silently.
Desperately.

You Feel Gross about This Instinct

Immediately after the comparison, shame shows up
swinging.
"What the fuck is wrong with you?"
"Why can't you just be compassionate?"

Here's the answer:
You're not cruel.

You're conditioned.

You learned care was conditional.
You learned help came late.
You learned being "fine" meant being invisible.
That doesn't vanish just because you know better now.

Support Spaces Can Accidentally Reward Competition

This part is uncomfortable but real.
Sometimes the room goes quiet for the most dramatic story.
Sometimes empathy flows toward extremity.
Sometimes stability gets overlooked.
No one means to create a hierarchy.
But your body notices patterns before your values intervene.
And once you see it, you can't unsee it.

You're Afraid That If Someone Else Hurts More, You'll Lose Your Place

Not your place as a person.
Your place as someone allowed to need help.
When someone else's pain eclipses yours, something panics:
"Do I still get to exist here?"

That's not jealousy.
That's fear of erasure.

You Start Policing Your Own Pain

You downplay.
Then overcorrect.

Then downplay again.

You ask yourself:
- "Is this bad enough to mention?"
- "Am I allowed to struggle today?"
- "Am I taking up space I didn't earn?"

Comparison broke your barometer.
Now you don't trust it.

You're Not Competing for Suffering, You're Competing for Care

Let's say this cleanly:
You are not trying to win pain.
You are trying to secure safety.
When care feels finite, pain becomes a résumé.
And résumés invite comparison.

This Is What Happens When Systems Fail to Be Consistent

In a world where support was reliable,
no one would need to compare.
In a world where pain was believed without escalation,
no one would hoard proof.

Competition grows in the cracks of inadequate care.

You Can Feel This without Liking It

You don't have to endorse this instinct.
You don't have to act on it.
You don't have to be proud of it.
You just have to admit it exists.
Pretending it doesn't only gives it more power.

This doesn't end with 'everyone's pain is valid' stitched
on a pillow.
You already know that.

It ends with context:
When survival required evidence, comparison became a
survival skill.

If you feel competitive about suffering…
If someone else's pain makes you quietly inventory
your own…
If you hate that part of yourself…
You're not heartless.
You're not narcissistic.
You're not broken.
You learned to protect your right to care in a system
that made pain prove itself.

And that instinct didn't disappear just because you grew
insight.

When pain had to compete to be seen,
comparison became a language of survival,
and unlearning it takes more than shame.

You never needed to win suffering to deserve care.
You just needed someone to see you before it got that
bad.

Chapter 33
Envy toward People Who Are Okay

The quiet, ugly jealousy no one claps for.

Let's say the thing you're supposed to swallow with a smile:
"Sometimes I envy people who are okay."

Not "Instagram okay."
Not "Lying through their teeth okay."
Actually okay.

The kind of okay that doesn't require planning exits, rehearsing conversations,
or negotiating with your own brain before leaving the house.

And before you clutch your pearls, no, I don't wish them harm.

I don't want their lives to implode.
I don't want to "take away" their peace.
I just want to know what it feels like to wake up without dread as a baseline setting.

What "Okay" Looks Like From the Outside

They wake up tired, not defeated.
They feel sad, not annihilated.
They have problems that end instead of mutating.
They get stressed and then,

this part is wild,

they recover.

They don't scan rooms.
They don't overanalyze tone.
They don't flinch when someone says, "Can we talk?"
They don't spend half their energy bracing for impact
that never comes.

They just…live.

Casually.

Like their nervous system didn't grow up in a combat
zone.

It's Not Jealousy. It's Grief in a Trench Coat

This isn't about wanting what they have.
It's about mourning what you don't.

You're not mad they're okay.
You're grieving that you're not.
You're grieving the ease.
The simplicity.
The unremarkable peace of not having to work this hard
just to exist.

And grief is sneaky like that, it shows up as envy
because envy is easier to admit than I lost something I
never even got.

The Rage of "Why Them?"

Here's the part you don't say out loud:
"Why them?"
"Why do they get a brain that shuts off at night?"
"Why do they get safety without strategy?"
"Why do they get to be mediocre and fine?"

You don't think you deserve more than them.
You just want the same starting line.

Instead,
you got dropped into the race barefoot,
already bleeding,
with a backpack full of trauma and no map.

And you're supposed to clap for everyone else's
milestones like you're not exhausted just standing
upright.

When Their Advice Makes It Worse

Nothing fuels envy like unsolicited wisdom from
someone who has never been there.
"Have you tried letting it go?"
"Don't overthink it."
"You worry too much."

Oh my God.
You're right.
I'll just uninstall my nervous system.
My bad.

They think your suffering is a mindset problem.
You know it's a wiring issue.
They think peace is a choice.
You know it's a privilege.

You Hate That You Notice It

You don't want to be this person.
You don't want to resent their joy,
their ease,
their lightness.

You don't want to feel bitter watching someone move
through life without armor.

So you shame yourself for it.

Be happy for them.
Don't compare.

It's not a competition.
And that shame just adds another layer to the pile
you're already carrying.

Being "Okay" Is Invisible until you're not

People who are okay don't know they're okay.
That's the cruel part.
They don't see it as luck.
They don't see it as access.
They think it's normal.

They don't realize how much of their energy is unspent.
How much capacity they have simply because their
brain isn't constantly putting out fires.
They don't know what it costs you to do the same
things effortlessly.

And they don't mean to be cruel about it.
They just don't know.

Envy doesn't mean you're a Bad Person

It means you're tired.
It means you've been living in survival mode so long
that peace feels fictional.
It means you can recognize what you were denied
without turning it into self-hatred.

Envy is what happens when injustice has nowhere to
go.
It's not malice.
It's math.

There Is No Resolution Where This Stops Hurting

I'm not going to tell you to reframe this.
I'm not going to tell you to practice gratitude until it
disappears.
I'm not going to say "everyone struggles" like struggle
is evenly distributed.

Some people are okay.
Some people aren't.

And the difference isn't always effort,
or mindset,
or moral superiority.

Sometimes it's just wiring.
Sometimes it's timing.
Sometimes it's what happened,
and what didn't,
when no one was watching.

If you feel envy toward people who are okay…
If their ease feels like an insult to your exhaustion…
If their normal makes your survival feel unfair…

You're not cruel.
You're not small.
You're not broken.

You're someone who has been carrying too much
for too long

and can still recognize what peace looks like,
even from the outside.

It's okay to envy what you never got.
It doesn't make you a bad person.
It makes you honest about the cost of living this way.

And honesty, in a world that keeps pretending this is
equal,
is its own quiet act of defiance.

Chapter 34
Why People Only like You When You're Improving

Progress is the only palatable version of you.

People don't like you.
They like improvement.
They like you when you're trending upward,
when your pain has a narrative,
when your suffering comes with a beginning, middle,
and a promising "getting better" energy they can root
for like a Netflix redemption series.

They like you when you can say, "I'm working on it,"
not when you say, "This is still here."
They like you when you're improving,
because improvement is reassuring.

Stagnation is terrifying.

The Applause Is Conditional

Notice how the room changes.
When you say:
"I'm doing better."

People smile.
Relax.
Lean in.

When you say:
"I'm struggling again."
People stiffen.
Look at the clock.
Suggest yoga.
You don't become less likable because you're hurting.

You become inconvenient.
Your pain stops being inspirational and starts being a
reminder that recovery isn't linear,
and nobody wants to sit with that.

Growth Is Entertaining. Maintenance Is Boring

Everyone loves the comeback.
No one loves the maintenance phase.

They love:
- The breakthrough.
- The diagnosis.
- The "aha" moment.
- The first few weeks of hope.

They do not love:
- The plateaus.
- The relapses.
- The long, flat middle.
- The years where nothing resolves.

Maintenance doesn't give people a role.
There's no cheerleading script for "still managing."

So they drift.

You Become a Project, Not a Person

When you're improving, people can root for you.

They can:
- Give advice.
- Offer encouragement.
- Feel useful.

When you stop improving, they feel helpless.

And instead of tolerating that discomfort,
they quietly step back.

Because a person who doesn't "get better"
threatens the illusion that effort guarantees outcomes.

Your Pain Is Welcome Only If It Has an Expiration Date

People don't want to hear:
"This might always be part of my life."

They want:
"This phase taught me something."
"This made me stronger."
"This is almost over."

They want pain with a return policy.

When your suffering overstays its welcome,
they stop offering seats.

Improvement Makes Them Feel Safe

This isn't always cruelty.
Sometimes it's fear.

Your continued struggle forces people to confront:
- Their own fragility.
- Their limited control.
- The lie that healing is guaranteed.

So they gravitate toward you when you're improving,

because improvement reassures them that things work
out if you just try hard enough.

And when you're not improving?
You become a living contradiction.

The Subtle Withdrawal Nobody Talks About

It's not dramatic abandonment.
It's quieter than that.

Texts slow.
Invitations fade.
Concern turns into advice turns into silence.

You're not pushed away.
You're gently deprioritized.
And the message lands anyway:
Come back when you're easier.

You Start Performing Recovery

This is where it gets self-erasing.
You learn which version of you is welcome.

So you:
- Downplay symptoms.
- Highlight progress.
- Hide relapses.
- Smile through exhaustion.

You say "I'm okay" not because it's true,
but because it keeps people around.

You become a PR manager for your own suffering.

Relapse Feels like Social Failure

It's not just that you're hurting again.
It's that you feel like you've disappointed everyone.
Like you broke an unspoken contract:
"We supported you, so why aren't you better?"

You internalize it.
You blame yourself.
You stop being honest.
Because honesty costs you connection.

They Don't Want the Whole Truth, They Want a Timeline

People ask:
"How are you?"

What they mean:
"Are you done yet?"

They don't know how to be present without a finish line.
They don't know how to love someone who might always be managing something.

So they attach their affection to progress.

This Isn't About You Being Unlovable

It's about people being deeply uncomfortable with unresolved pain.

Your worth didn't decrease.
Their tolerance just ran out.
That's not a reflection of your value.
It's a reflection of how conditional support often is.

If people only show up when you're improving…
If support fades the moment progress slows…
If your pain is tolerated only when it's temporary…
You're not imagining it.
You're not failing.
You're not "doing healing wrong."

You've learned the ugly truth:
People are better at cheering growth than sitting with
reality.

There's no fix here.
No lesson.
No advice about finding better people.

Just this:
You are allowed to exist even when you're not
improving.
You are allowed to be loved without performing
recovery.

And if that makes people uncomfortable?
That discomfort is not your responsibility.
It never was.

Chapter 35
When People Say "Reach Out" But Don't Mean You

"Reach out if you need anything."

They say it like a blessing.
Like a spell.
Like a little moral air freshener they hang in the room
so nobody has to smell the reality of being mentally ill.

It's the emotional equivalent of,
"Let's do lunch sometime,"
except the lunch is your nervous system actively eating
itself and the reservation is never confirmed.

Because what they actually mean is:

Reach out...
...but not like that.
Reach out...
...but keep it cute.
Reach out...
...but don't make me responsible for anything more
than a heart emoji and one inspirational sentence I stole
from Pinterest.

They mean the version of you who is sad, but articulate.
Vulnerable, but contained.
Honest, but not honest enough to trigger their own
discomfort.

They do not mean:

The you who is spiraling and repeating yourself because you can't get your brain to land.

The you who is angry and sharp and not "asking nicely."

The you who doesn't know what help looks like and might need more than "Have you tried breathing?"

The you who is not improving on a schedule that keeps other people comfortable.

And when you finally do reach out?

The tone shifts.
The air changes.

It's like you walked into their "supportive friend" stage play and accidentally delivered your lines from the real script.

Support Culture Is Mostly Performance Art

People love the idea of support.

Support looks good on them.
Support makes them feel like a good person without requiring any inconvenient behavior.

Support is a slogan.
A repost.
A candle emoji.
A hotline graphic.

A little "checking in <3" text they can send while still watching Netflix.

Real support is:
- Messy.
- Inconvenient.
- Repetitive.
- Time-consuming.
- Unresolved.

Real support doesn't end after one conversation.
It doesn't wrap up.
It doesn't hit a satisfying emotional conclusion where everyone learns a lesson and then goes to brunch.

So most people don't actually want to do support.
They want to signal it.

Like a yard sign.

"Reach Out" Comes With Fine Print

Their version of "reach out" has terms and conditions.

Reach out:
Politely.
Briefly.
During business hours.
In a tone that doesn't scare them.
With a clear request they can fulfill in under ten minutes.
With visible improvement within a reasonable time frame so they can feel successful.

Do not reach out:
At night.
More than once.
When you're incoherent.
When you're not sure what you need.
When you need follow-up.
When you're still struggling next week.
When your pain reminds them that they are also fragile,
mortal, and one bad month away from losing it.

That's not support.

That's customer service with a closing time.

The Text You Regret Sending

There is a specific humiliation that comes from finally
reaching out.

You type the message.
Delete it.
Rewrite it softer.
Add an apology like you're requesting a refund from a
company you don't want to anger.

"Sorry to bother you."
"Sorry, I know you're busy."
"Sorry, it's not that bad."
"It's fine if you can't respond."

You hit send with a shaking thumb.

And then...

Nothing.

Unread.
Seen with no reply.
Or the classic: "Omg sorry just seeing this now" three
days later, as if your crisis politely waited in the lobby
like it had an appointment.

You don't just feel ignored.

You feel stupid for believing them.

"Have You Talked to a Therapist?" and Other Ways to Say "Not Me"

Nothing makes you feel more alone than reaching out
and being redirected like a broken appliance.

"Have you tried therapy?"
"Maybe you should talk to a professional."
"I don't know what to say."
"That sounds hard."

Cool.
Neither do I.
That's why I reached out.

Also, respectfully:
If therapy was that easy to access, half of us wouldn't
be raw-dogging existence with a jittery nervous system
and a playlist called PLEASE KEEP ME ALIVE
UNTIL FRIDAY.

Sometimes it's not that people are cruel.

They're just terrified of being needed.
Unskilled at holding pain.
Allergic to discomfort.

And addicted to solutions.

But the impact is the same:
You reached out.
You did the brave thing.
And you learned the worst lesson possible…

Support is conditional.

The Cruel Math of Emotional Labor

Here's the unspoken rule:

The more often you struggle, the less patience people
have.

At first:
"I'm here for you."

Later:
"Have you tried journaling?"

Eventually:
Silence.

Because long-term pain makes people uncomfortable.
And discomfort is something they expect you to
manage, even while you're actively malfunctioning.

Your pain has a shelf life.

And once it expires, you become a burden instead of a
person.

Support Turns into Surveillance

Sometimes the support that shows up feels worse.

Check-ins that feel like monitoring.
Concern that feels like obligation.
Advice you didn't ask for.
Pressure to get better so they can relax.

You can feel the unspoken panic:

"Please improve so I can stop worrying."
"Please become manageable again."
"Please stop reminding me that I can't fix this."

So you learn to perform recovery.

You say, "I'm doing better,"
when what you mean is,
"I don't want you to disappear."

You add jokes so they don't feel helpless.
You minimize the scary parts so they don't label you
"too much."

You Start Editing Your Pain for Public Consumption

After enough non-responses, you adapt.

You stop saying the real thing.
You stop saying the worst thing.
You stop saying anything that might require someone to
show up in a way that costs them something.

You learn the acceptable version of suffering:
Sad but not suicidal.
Anxious but still functional.
Struggling but still polite.
Depressed but still replying "lol" so no one feels
responsible.

You don't stop reaching out because you don't need
help.

You stop reaching out because you learned the cost of
honesty.

"You Should Have Said Something" Is the Final Insult

This line should be illegal.

Because you did say something.

You whispered.
You hinted.
You tested the waters.
You tried to make it digestible.
You reached with a hand that was shaking.

They just didn't catch you.

Or they did, and froze.
Or they did, and looked away.
Or they did, and decided it was "above their pay grade,"
which is a wild thing to say about a human being you
supposedly care about.

So they rewrite history to protect themselves from guilt:

"Why didn't you reach out?"
"We had no idea."
"I wish you would've told us."

And you're sitting there like:
I did.
You just didn't mean me.

Better Friends Aren't the Answer

I'm not going to tell you to "find your people."
I'm not going to promise "the right ones will stay."

Sometimes they don't.
Sometimes the bench is empty.
Sometimes the only person who answers is a crisis line
and your own bitter willpower.

That is not a reflection of your worth.

It's a reflection of how thin support culture actually is.

If you stopped reaching out…
If asking for help taught you not to ask again…
If "support" felt like a mirage that disappeared the
second you actually needed it…

You're not dramatic.
You're not bitter.
You're not "too much."

You learned from experience.

And that learning hurts.

There's no moral lesson here.
No net solution.
No "keep trying" speech.

Just this:
Being told to reach out, and discovering there's no one
on the other end, is its own kind of trauma.

And surviving that silence doesn't make you strong.

It just makes you quiet.

Chapter 36
Relationships When You Don't Trust Safety

Love feels like temporary permission.
I don't do relationships assuming safety.
I do them assuming temporary permission.
Temporary permission to be seen.
Temporary permission to be wanted.
Temporary permission to exist before someone changes
their mind, gets bored, gets overwhelmed, or gets close
enough to hurt me by accident.

Love doesn't feel like home.
It feels like a lease with fine print I haven't read yet and
a landlord who can knock whenever they want.

People say, "Just be yourself."
Cute.
Myself is a collection of contingency plans wearing
eyeliner.

I don't enter relationships thinking,
"This could last."
I enter thinking,
"How bad will it hurt when it ends?"

Not if.
When.

Attachment Issues Don't Look Like Not Wanting Love

Here's the lie people love to tell:
"If you're afraid of closeness, you must not want
intimacy."

Bullshit.

I want it desperately.
I just don't trust it to stay safe once it arrives.

I don't fear connection.
I fear the price of connection.

Because closeness historically meant:
Being seen.
Being needed.
Being depended on.
Being blamed.
Being punished for having needs.
Being left once I relaxed.

So now my body reacts before my heart gets a vote.
I don't fall in love.
I brace for impact.

I Don't Relax Into Relationships, I Manage Them

I don't rest in connection.
I monitor it.
I track tone shifts like a crime scene analyst.
I notice response times.
I reread messages like I'm decoding a hostage letter.
Why was that shorter?
Why no emoji?
Why did they take four hours instead of two?
Did I say something three days ago that they're just
now resenting?

I'm never just in the relationship.
I'm overseeing it.

Because safety has a history of being revoked without
warning.

Calm Feels Suspicious. Chaos Feels Familiar

When someone is distant, my brain goes:
"Oh. Familiar terrain."
When someone is warm, my brain goes:
"What do you want?"

Consistency makes me uneasy.
Care without conditions feels fake.
Kindness feels like bait.

I wait for the reveal.

Everyone has one.
They always do.

I trust patterns more than promises.
Words are cheap.
Silence is louder.

I Test People without Meaning To

Not consciously.
Not maliciously.
Strategically.

I pull back to see if they chase.
I go quiet to see if they notice.
I stay half-available so I don't fall too hard.

If they leave, I get to say, "See? I knew it."
If they stay, I panic harder.
Because now there's something to lose.

Relationships become exams I never studied for.
A delayed text becomes abandonment.
A bad mood becomes my fault.
A disagreement becomes the beginning of the end.

I don't ask what's happening.
I assume.
And my assumptions are always worst-case, because
hope feels reckless.

Sometimes I Ruin It On Purpose

Not because I enjoy chaos.
Because I prefer predictable pain.

If I end it first,
If I push them away,
If I make myself unlovable,
At least I'm not surprised when it falls apart.

Rejection hurts less when you choreograph it.
Self-sabotage feels like control.
Control feels safer than trust.

I Love With One Foot out the Door

I crave intimacy and immediately plan my escape route.
I don't attach.
I brace.
I keep emotional exits unlocked.
I love with one foot out the door because leaving on my
own terms feels safer than being left.

People think I'm afraid of commitment.
I'm not.

I'm afraid of being trapped in a dynamic where I give everything and still end up abandoned, blamed, or erased.

I'm afraid of relaxing and paying for it later.

I'm Actually Very Good at Relationships (And It's Exhausting)

I anticipate needs.
I read moods.
I adapt fast.
I take responsibility for things that aren't mine.
I'm emotionally agile and completely drained.
Because loving when you don't trust safety means
you're preparing for loss while pretending you're fine.

I don't ask for reassurance, I ration it.
I don't ask for clarity, I infer it.
I don't explode, I implode.

I blame myself.
I replay everything.
I decide I misjudged, misunderstood, miscalculated.

Because if it's my fault, at least the chaos makes sense.

Receiving Love Is Harder Than Giving It

Giving feels active.
Receiving feels like owing.
So I over-give.
I become indispensable.

Being useful feels safer than being wanted.
Being needed feels less risky than being cherished.

Compliments make me flinch.
Commitment feels like a liability.
When someone says, "I care about you," my brain
hears,
"…until you disappoint me."

I Mistake Anxiety for Chemistry

I mistake intensity for connection.
I mistake unpredictability for depth.
I mistake chaos for passion.

Calm feels boring.
Chaos feels familiar.

My nervous system trusts what it recognizes,
not what's actually healthy.

People call me too much or too distant.
Needy if I reach.
Cold if I pull back.
I can't win.

I Didn't Learn How to Be Loved

I learned how to survive attachment.
Those are not the same skill set.

I didn't learn safety.
I learned vigilance.

I didn't learn trust.
I learned pattern recognition.

I didn't learn rest.
I learned readiness.

This Is Not About Fixing Attachment Styles

This isn't about healing your attachment style.
It's not about choosing better partners or friends.
It's not about bravely trusting again.

It is just this:
When safety has been conditional, inconsistent, or
weaponized, love never feels simple.

It feels like exposure.
It feels like risk.
It feels like standing unarmored in a place where you
learned armor was required.

And I still try.
Not because I'm healed.
Not because I'm fearless.
But because even with every alarm blaring, some part
of me still wants connection badly enough to step
closer, while keeping one eye on the exit.

That's not dysfunction.
That's what loving looks like when trust was never
guaranteed.

And sometimes, even with all of this?
Being alone with your own head feels worse.

So you risk it.
Again.
And again.
Knowing exactly how much it might cost.

Chapter 37
Boundaries Feel like Violence (Even when they're not)

"Just set a boundary" sounds like a threat.

Every time someone says, "Just set a boundary," my nervous system hears, "Start a controlled burn and stand inside it."

Not a polite disagreement.
Not a healthy adult conversation.
A felony.

Sirens in my chest.
Stomach drops out like an elevator cable snapped.
Hands shaking like I just did something irreversible.

Boundaries don't feel calm.
They don't feel grounded.
They don't feel empowering.

They feel like impact.
Like slamming a door.
Like cutting someone off mid-sentence.
Like choosing violence, even when all you said was, "I can't do that."

And my body reacts like I just punched someone's grandma.

Why "No" Never Felt Neutral

I didn't learn no as a complete sentence.
I learned it as a trigger.

No meant punishment.
No meant withdrawal.
No meant escalation.
No meant someone getting colder, louder, meaner, or
gone.
No meant consequences.

So when people say, "You're allowed to say no,"
my nervous system laughs hysterically
and starts packing a go-bag.
Because historically, no was not empowerment.
It was danger.

Boundaries Don't Feel Like Self-Respect. They Feel Like Provocation

When I set a boundary, my brain doesn't think,
"This is healthy."
It thinks:
"You've just activated something."
"Something bad is coming."
"Prepare to manage fallout."

Immediate consequences.
Delayed consequences.
Mystery consequences scheduled for 2 a.m. when I
replay the conversation for the 400th time.

Boundaries feel violent because they interrupt survival
patterns that once kept me alive.
People-pleasing wasn't a flaw, it was armor.
Over-explaining wasn't insecurity, it was damage
control.
Self-abandonment wasn't weakness, it was strategy.
So when I stop doing those things, my body panics.

If I don't manage everyone else's emotions, who will?
If I don't smooth this over, what happens next?
If I choose myself, who pays for it?

The Guilt Shows Up Fully Formed

The guilt doesn't trickle in later.
It arrives immediately.
Fully dressed.
Carrying receipts.
"You're being selfish."
"You're overreacting."
"You're making this harder than it needs to be."
"They're going to be hurt because of you."

Never mind whether the request was unreasonable.
Never mind whether you're exhausted.
Never mind whether saying yes would quietly wreck
you.

The guilt doesn't care about facts.
It cares about conditioning.

So you don't just say no.
You justify it.

You soften it.
You apologize.
You write a whole fucking dissertation.
"I'm so sorry, I just can't right now because…"

Because you were taught that refusal required
explanation.
That boundaries had to be polite, gentle, palatable, and
impossible to argue with.
And even then, you still feel like an asshole.

When Someone Reacts Badly, Your Body Says: "Proof."

When someone pushes back on a boundary, your
nervous system goes:
"See?"
"You hurt them."
"You caused this."
"This is why we don't do this."

Even when their reaction is manipulative.
Even when it's disproportionate.
Even when it's absolute bullshit.

Your body doesn't analyze fairness.
It panics.
Because conflict used to cost you safety.

Boundaries feel aggressive when you were trained to be
small.
They feel rude when you were trained to be grateful.

They feel threatening when you were trained to survive
by disappearing.

Why you'd Rather Be Resentful than Rejected

Here's the part nobody likes to admit:
Sometimes you don't set boundaries because
resentment feels safer than rejection.

You'll take exhaustion.
You'll take irritation.
You'll take quiet, simmering anger.
Because those feelings are familiar.
Rejection isn't.

So you say yes.
Then you resent them.
Then you resent yourself.
Then you feel guilty for resenting anyone at all.
It's a beautifully efficient trauma loop.

"You've Changed" Is Not the Insult They Think It Is

When you finally do set a boundary, some people will
be pissed.
Not everyone.
Just the ones who benefited from your lack of
boundaries.

They'll say:
"You've changed."
"You're selfish now."

"You're dramatic."
"I miss the old you."

What they mean is:
"I miss when you were easier to access."

That doesn't mean your boundary is wrong.
It means it worked.

Even When Nothing Happens, Your Body Still Waits

Even when no one yells.
Even when no one leaves.
Even when no one explodes.
Your body still braces.
Because the absence of immediate fallout doesn't equal safety to a trauma-trained nervous system.

It just means not yet.
So you sit there, heart pounding, waiting for the other shoe to drop,
even if the shoe never existed.

When Boundaries Feel Like Violence

This isn't about scripts.
Or confidence.
Or standing tall in your worth.

It's about telling the truth:
Boundaries can feel violent to people who learned survival through self-erasure.

They feel like danger even when they're healthy.
They feel like loss even when they're protective.
They feel like cruelty even when they're necessary.
And still, you set them.

Shakily.
Imperfectly.
With your heart racing and your brain screaming.

Not because it feels good.
But because somewhere along the way, you realized
that constantly betraying yourself was its own kind of
violence.
And you've already survived enough of that.

Unlearning what once kept you safe doesn't feel
peaceful.

It feels like going against muscle memory.
And sometimes, making the fear make sense is the
closest thing to relief you get.

Chapter 38
Grief Doesn't End, It Just Changes Outfits

Grief does not move on.
It doesn't resolve.
It doesn't respect your timeline, your progress, or the
fact that it's been years and you're supposed to be
normal now.

Grief doesn't pack a box.
It doesn't leave a forwarding address.
It doesn't give a single shit that you're tired of carrying
it.
It just changes outfits and shows up anyway.

At first, it's obvious.
Loud.
Heavy.
Black clothes, red eyes, casseroles you didn't ask for.

You cry in public.
You forget how to function.
People nod sympathetically and treat you like a
wounded animal that might bite.

Then time passes.
And grief swaps black for business casual.
It blends in.
It shows up as irritability.
As exhaustion.
As a bad mood you can't trace back to anything
specific.

You think, "What the fuck is wrong with me today?"
Nothing new.
Just grief in a hoodie.

Grief Is Not a Straight Line. It's a Drunk Spiral with No Apology.

People love the stages of grief.
Denial.
Anger.
Bargaining.
Depression.
Acceptance.

Cute.

In reality, grief is a feral raccoon that breaks into your house at random intervals and knocks over your emotional furniture.

You think you're fine for months.
Functioning.
Even laughing.

Then you smell their shampoo in a grocery store aisle and suddenly you're crying over cantaloupe like you've completely lost your mind.

You didn't "go backwards."
Grief just circled back like it forgot something.

Anniversaries Are Emotional Ambushes

The obvious dates at least give you a warning.
Birthdays.
Death dates.
Holidays.

You can brace.
Lower expectations.

Say, "Oh right. That's today."
But grief loves the sneaky ones.
A smell that shouldn't matter.
A song you forgot existed.
A throwaway comment that detonates something
ancient in your chest.

Suddenly you're crying in the cereal aisle because
Captain Crunch reminded you of someone who no
longer exists and your nervous system decided now was
the time.

Your body remembers dates your brain pretends not to.
Grief keeps a calendar you don't have access to.

Delayed Grief Is a Real Kick in the Teeth

Sometimes you don't fall apart right away.
Sometimes you survive first.
You plan funerals.
You take care of other people.
You hold everything together.
Everyone applauds your strength.

Grief notices.
Grief waits.

Then, months or years later,
when your life finally calms down,
when you're no longer in crisis mode,
your nervous system clocks in like:
"Cool. You're not actively surviving anymore. Now we
can feel everything you postponed."

You didn't ignore grief.
You deferred it.

You weren't broken back then.
You were busy.
So now you fall apart later.
Over things you "should be over."
You're not weak.
You're late.

Grief Is Love with Nowhere to Go

Here's the part no one wants to sit with:
Grief isn't just missing someone.
It's all the love you still have with no place to put it.
The jokes you don't get to make.
The updates you don't get to share.
The comfort you don't get to receive.

So the love turns inward.
And heavy.
And sharp.
And sometimes bitter.

People say shit like, "At least you have good
memories."

Cool.

Memories are haunted.
They don't comfort.
They ambush.

You Carry Ghosts into Adulthood

Grief isn't only about death.
It's about childhoods you didn't get.
Versions of yourself that didn't survive.

Parents who were physically present but emotionally unavailable.
People who are alive but unreachable.
There are losses that never got funerals.
So no one told you it was okay to mourn them.

You swallowed it.
Adapted.
Called it "moving on."

Congratulations.
You just gave grief a longer shelf life.

Loss grows up with you.
What hurt at ten hurts differently at forty.
What you didn't understand then becomes unbearable once you finally do.

You become an adult with invisible passengers.
Some days they're quiet.
Some days they grab the wheel.

People Get Tired of Your Grief Before You Do

There's a socially acceptable grief window.
After that?
You're supposed to be "better."

People stop asking.
They change the subject.
They get uncomfortable when you mention the dead.
As if loving someone past their expiration date is inconvenient.

So you learn to grieve quietly.
Again.

Grief Can Be Angry, Petty, and Ugly

Not all grief is poetic.
Sometimes it's rage.
Sometimes it's jealousy.
Sometimes it's resentment toward people who still have
what you lost.
Sometimes it's bitterness wrapped in shame because
you're not supposed to feel that way.

But you do.
Because grief is not polite.

Healing Is a Lie People Tell to Feel Better

Grief doesn't heal like a wound.
It scabs.
It scars.
It aches when the weather changes.

You don't "move on."
You move with it.

Some days it's manageable.
Some days it feels like dragging a corpse behind you
emotionally and pretending that's normal.

Grief doesn't make you stronger.
It makes you heavier.
More cautious.
More aware of how fragile everything actually is.

Which is not inspirational.
It's just honest.

There's no moment where grief ends.
There's just the slow, quiet integration of loss into who
you are.
You don't stop missing.
You don't stop loving.
You don't stop carrying it.
You just learn how to stand with the weight.

If your grief still sneaks up on you…
If years later it still knocks the wind out of you…
If you feel broken because it never fully left…
You're not failing.
You're remembering.

Grief doesn't mean you're stuck.
It means something mattered enough to leave
permanent damage.

Grief doesn't end.
It just changes outfits, and keeps walking beside you,
whether you like it or not.

And you live anyway.
Not because it gets easier.
But because the alternative doesn't exist.

So you carry your ghosts.
Not gracefully.
Not quietly.
Just…continuously.

Part VII: Where This Actually Came From

Chapter 39
Anger at Parents Who "Did Their Best"

"Your parents did their best."

Ah yes.
The sacred phrase.
The emotional duct tape slapped over entire childhoods
like that sentence magically fixes structural damage.

It's said gently.
Defensively.
Like a period at the end of a conversation you were
never allowed to finish.

I hate that phrase.

Not because it's always false.
But because it's used like a gag order.

Once someone says they did their best, you're expected
to stop feeling.
Stop asking questions.
Stop being angry.
Close the file.
Accept the damage as an unfortunate side effect of
good intentions.

Case dismissed.

"Their Best" Doesn't Undo the Damage

Here's the thing no one wants to say out loud:
Someone can do their best
and still fuck you up.
Someone can love you

and still be unsafe.
Someone can be overwhelmed, traumatized, struggling
and still neglect, dismiss, abandon, or emotionally harm
you.

"Best" is not the same as enough.
And it sure as hell isn't the same as okay.

Intent does not cancel impact.
Effort does not erase outcomes.
Love does not automatically teach safety.

Those truths don't cancel each other out.
They sit in the same room and glare at each other.

People Use "They Did Their Best" to Shut You Up
Let's be honest.

That phrase isn't for you.
It's for everyone else.

It's used to:
- Avoid discomfort.
- End the conversation.
- Protect a narrative.
- Make your anger look unreasonable.

Once they did their best is invoked,
you're expected to forgive,
heal,
and move on quietly,
preferably without making anyone else examine their
own family dynamics.

No more grief.
No more rage.

No more inconvenient truths.

You're Not Angry Because You Expected Perfection

You didn't need perfect parents.

You needed:
- Safety.
- Consistency.
- Protection.
- Someone who noticed when you were drowning.

You needed repair when harm happened.

Instead, you got explanations.
Excuses.
Silence.
Or denial wrapped in good intentions.

That's what you're angry about.

Love without Skill Still Wounds

This is the nuance people hate.
They may have loved you.
They may have tried.
They may have been doing the best they could with what they had.

And still…
They taught you fear.
They modeled chaos.
They normalized neglect, volatility, or emotional absence.

You can understand why
and still be furious about what.
Those things are not mutually exclusive.

You Were Asked to Be the Bigger Person Too Early

You learned to empathize upward.
To understand their stress.
Their trauma.
Their limitations.
You carried compassion before you had language for
your own pain.

And now, as an adult, people expect you to keep doing
that.
To keep protecting them from your truth.
You're tired of being bigger.
You were the child.
And now you're the one paying for therapy, meds,
coping skills, and a lifetime subscription to
hypervigilance.

No parade.
No acknowledgment.
Just invoices.

Your Anger Is About Accountability, Not Revenge

You're not asking to punish them.
You're asking for acknowledgment.
For someone to say:
Yes. That hurt you.
Yes. It mattered.
Yes. It wasn't okay, even if it wasn't intentional.
And when that never comes, anger fills the space where
repair should have been.

"They Did Their Best" Erases Your Right to Grieve

That phrase quietly suggests:
- You shouldn't be this affected.
- Your pain is excessive.
- Your trauma is inconvenient.

It asks you to be grateful instead of honest.
That's how anger calcifies.

You're allowed to Be Angry at People You Still Love

This is another taboo.
You can love your parents and still resent the hell out of
what they failed to give you.

Love doesn't require amnesia.
Connection doesn't require absolution.
Family doesn't cancel accountability.
Anger doesn't mean you hate them.
It means something unresolved still hurts.

You Don't Owe Them Emotional Redemption

You don't owe:
- Forgiveness on demand.
- Closure for their comfort.
- A healed version of yourself that proves they
  weren't "that bad."

Your healing is not a retroactive character reference for
them.

Some Parents Want Credit without Repair

Here's the quiet truth:
Some parents want recognition for trying without
facing the consequences of how they failed.

They want absolution without accountability.
Understanding without responsibility.
Peace without repair.
You're allowed to say no to that deal.

This Anger Is Old. And it's earned.

It didn't show up overnight.

It grew every time you were:
- Not protected.
- Not believed.
- Not prioritized.
- Asked to adapt instead of being cared for.

Anger is what remains when grief was never given
room.

No Forgiveness…Just Naming the Wound.

This doesn't end with reconciliation.
It does not end with they did the best they could.

It ends with the truth:
Their best still left you with scars.

And being angry about that doesn't make you cruel.
It makes you honest about what it cost you to grow up
in an environment that required you to be resilient
instead of protected.

If you're angry at parents who "did their best"…
If that phrase makes something sharp rise in you…
If you feel guilty for not being more understanding…
You're not ungrateful.
You're not rewriting history.
You're not asking for too much.
You're acknowledging that love without safety still
harms, and that harm doesn't disappear just because no
one meant it.

Sometimes the most radical thing you can do is stop
protecting the story and finally tell your own.
And that, uncomfortable as it is, is the only kind of
honesty that actually changes anything.

Chapter 40
Trauma Made Me like This

I didn't wake up one day and choose hypervigilance, emotional whiplash, trust issues, and a personality held together with sarcasm and duct tape.

Trauma made me like this.

Not in a cute, "character development" way.
In a "my nervous system learned war tactics before it learned rest way."

People love to ask, "Why are you like this?"
Like there's a tidy origin story that won't make them uncomfortable.

Here it is:

Shit happened
Then more shit happened.
Then I adapted.

That's it.

Trauma doesn't politely damage one area and leave the rest intact.
It rewires.
It spreads.
It gets into places you didn't know were editable.

It turns your body into a threat-detection system with no off switch.
It turns love into something you approach sideways.
It turns calm into a red flag.

Trauma didn't make me stronger.
Trauma made me alert.

Trauma Isn't Just What Happened

People love to ask, "What happened to you?"
As if trauma is a single event with a date,
a villain,
and a closing argument.

Sometimes it was abuse.
Sometimes it was neglect.
Sometimes it was being praised only when you
performed and ignored when you needed comfort.
Sometimes it was growing up in a house where
emotions were inconvenient and silence was survival.
Sometimes it was a thousand tiny moments that taught
your nervous system one core lesson:

You are on your own.

So now your body believes that.
Even when you're not.

Trauma isn't just the bad thing.
It's the absence of safety when you needed it most.

Your Body Learned Before Your Brain Could Object

Here's the inconvenient truth:

You can forget trauma.
Your body cannot.

Your body keeps receipts like a petty accountant.

Your heart races before you know why.
Your stomach drops over nothing.
Your shoulders live up near your ears like they're
trying to escape your spine.

People say things like, "You're safe now."

Cool.

My nervous system missed that memo.

Because trauma doesn't live in logic.
It lives in reflex.

It's a door closing too loud.
It's a pause in a text conversation.
It's someone saying, "Can we talk?" in a neutral tone
that sends your pulse into the stratosphere.

Your body reacts first.
Your brain plays catch-up later.
And shame fills the gap in between.

Why You Overreact (Except you're not)

Trauma responses are deeply unglamorous.

They look like:

Shutting down during conflict.
Exploding over something small.
Needing reassurance and resenting yourself for it.
Reading rejection into neutral situations.
Freezing when you need to speak.
People-pleasing like it's an Olympic sport.

Then immediately judging yourself for all of it.
You call yourself dramatic.
Too sensitive.
Broken.

What you actually are is conditioned.

These reactions were learned.
They worked once.
They kept you alive.

They just didn't get the update that the danger changed.

Trauma Ruins Your Relationship with Time

No one warns you about this part.

Trauma collapses time.

Your body reacts to now like it's then.

That tone of voice?
That silence?
That look?

Your brain may know you're forty-four and standing in
your kitchen.

Your body is six.
Or twelve.
Or nineteen.
Back in it.
Bracing.

So you react bigger than the moment deserves.

Then you feel stupid for it.
Which adds shame.
Which deepens the spiral.
Which teaches your body it was right to panic in the
first place.

It's a closed loop from hell.

Trauma Skills That Look Like Personality Defects

Trauma teaches you skills that look like flaws to people
who never needed them.

Over-explaining?
That's threat mitigation.

People-pleasing?
That's survival math.

Dark humor?
That's emotional shock absorption.

Control issues?
That's what happens when unpredictability almost
killed you.

Hyper-independence?
That's learned abandonment prevention.

You didn't become like this because you wanted
attention.

You became like this because attention was either the
only way to stay safe, or the most punishing thing in the
room.

Calm Feels Fake, Crisis Feels Familiar

Here's another truth nobody likes:

Trauma makes you good in emergencies and feral in
quiet rooms.

You're calm when everything's on fire.
You fall apart when things finally slow down.

Because crisis feels familiar.
Stillness feels like a setup.

Your nervous system learned that bad things happen
when you let your guard down.

So rest feels suspicious.
Peace feels temporary.
Joy comes with a brace for impact.

People call this self-sabotage.

It's actually pattern recognition.

"Don't Let Your Past Define You" Is a Comfort Statement for Other People

People get weird when you say trauma shaped you.

They say things like:
"Don't let your past define you."
"That was so long ago."
"You can choose to move on."

As if your nervous system didn't learn its rules there.

As if memory lives politely in the brain instead of the body.
As if trauma is a story you tell instead of a reflex you feel.

Time does not heal trauma.
Safety does.
Consistency does.
And sometimes you didn't get those things.

Sometimes you got survival instead.

And survival leaves residue.

You Didn't Heal Wrong

Let's say this clearly:
You didn't heal wrong.
You healed enough to keep going.

Dissociation kept you sane.
Numbing out kept you functional.
Hypervigilance kept you alive.

The problem isn't that you still use them.
The problem is the world expects you to uninstall them like outdated software without acknowledging why they exist.

This Is the Part Where People Expect Forgiveness

I'm not going to tell you to forgive your trauma.
I'm not going to tell you to be grateful for it.
I'm not going to pretend it secretly gave you superpowers.

Sometimes trauma just fucked things up.

Sometimes it stole ease you'll never get back.
Sometimes it changed your nervous system
permanently.
Sometimes it made you sharp, closed, suspicious,
exhausting.

Pretending otherwise doesn't make you healed.

It just makes you quiet.

There is no closure.

There is no "and then I finally felt safe."

There is just this:

If your reactions feel bigger than the moment…
If your body panics before your brain can catch up…
If you feel broken for struggling with things other
people brush off…

Trauma made you like this.

Not weak.
Not dramatic.
Not defective.

Wired.

And maybe that wiring will soften someday.
Or maybe it won't.
Either way, you're not imagining it.
You're not failing.

You're living in a body that learned how to survive
something it shouldn't have had to.

That's not a happy ending.

It's just the truth.

And sometimes, finally naming it is the closest thing to
relief we get.

Part VIII: Identity Damage

Chapter 41
The Parts of You That Scare You the Most

There are parts of you that you don't introduce at parties.
Parts you keep locked in the basement with a chair under the doorknob.
Parts you pretend don't exist because if they did, you'd have to explain them,
and you are so tired of explaining yourself.

These are the parts that scare you.
Not because they're evil.
Because they're honest.

Meet the Parts You Tried to Kill Off

There's the angry one.
The numb one.
The impulsive one.
The one that wants to disappear.
The one that wants to burn everything down and start over.
The one that doesn't care if things end badly, as long as they end.

You call them:
- Toxic
- Dysfunctional
- Self-sabotaging
- A problem

You exile them because you were taught that good people don't feel like this.
But here's the uncomfortable truth:

Those parts didn't show up to ruin your life.
They showed up to protect it.

Self-Protection and Self-Destruction Wear the Same Coat

This is where things get messy.
The behaviors you hate most about yourself?
They probably saved you once.

Shutting down kept you safe.
Numbing out kept you functional.
Self-sabotage kept you from being blindsided.
Pulling away kept you from needing people who weren't safe.
Even the parts that flirt with destruction often started as escape plans.

They weren't trying to kill you.
They were trying to end the pain.
And yes, sometimes they overshot.
That doesn't make them villains.
It makes them desperate.

You Hate These Parts Because You Don't Trust Them

You're scared of what they might do.
You're scared that if you let them speak, they'll wreck everything.
You're scared that if you stop fighting them, they'll take over.
You're scared that this mess is the real you.
So you clamp down.
You control.
You suppress.

You shame.
And those parts don't go away.
They just get louder.

Exile Makes Monsters

Here's what nobody tells you:
The more you try to banish parts of yourself, the more
distorted they become.

Ignored pain doesn't dissolve.
Unheard needs don't disappear.
Silenced fear doesn't calm down.
It ferments.

So the parts you're afraid of start showing up sideways:
- In impulsive choices.
- In sudden rage.
- In numbing behaviors.
- In moments you don't recognize yourself.

And then you hate yourself more.
Which feeds the cycle.

Chef's kiss.

"Why Am I Like This?" Is the Wrong Question

The question isn't:
"What's wrong with me?"
It's:
"What did this part learn to do to survive?"

That question doesn't excuse harm.
It doesn't romanticize destruction.
It just tells the truth.

You didn't wake up one day and choose chaos.
Chaos was adaptive.
Until it wasn't.

Sitting with the Mess Feels Like Losing Control

People say "accept yourself" like it's a calm yoga pose.

It's not.

Accepting the scary parts feels like sitting in a room
with someone you don't fully trust.

You're alert.
You're tense.
You're waiting for something bad to happen.

Because you were taught that if you let go even a little,
everything would fall apart.

So you don't integrate.
You police.
And policing yourself is exhausting.

Integration Is Not Peaceful

Let's be clear:
Letting these parts exist does not feel like harmony.
It feels awkward.
Uncomfortable.
Disorienting.

It feels like admitting that you are not neat.
Not healed.
Not consistent.

It feels like acknowledging that you can want to live
and want to disappear in the same afternoon.

Which is terrifying if you've been chasing clarity your
whole life.

This Is Not About Loving Every Part of Yourself

I'm not going to tell you to love these parts.
Some of them are a lot.
Some of them are destructive.
Some of them have terrible ideas.

You don't have to like them.
You just have to stop pretending they're not there.

Because fighting yourself nonstop is not growth.
It's civil war.

No Resolution. Just Coexistence.

There is no moment where all your parts line up and
agree.
There's no final boss fight where the scary ones are
defeated.
There's just learning how to notice them without letting
them drive the car.
Learning how to say:
"I see you. I know why you're here. You don't get to
run everything anymore, but you're not being thrown
out."

That's not healing.
That's management.
And management is underrated.

If parts of you scare you…
If you're afraid of your own thoughts, urges, or
reactions…
If you've spent years trying to exile pieces of yourself
just to feel normal…
You're not broken.
You're fragmented in the way people get fragmented
when they survive things they weren't supposed to.

And no, sitting with the mess doesn't make it go away.
It just stops the war.

Sometimes.
On good days.

On bad days, it's still loud.

The parts of you that scare you the most didn't come to
destroy you.
They came because something once needed protecting.
And learning to sit with that truth is not beautiful.
It's just honest.
And honest is the best we've got.

Chapter 42
When This Becomes Your Personality (Against Your Will)

I didn't choose this brand.

I didn't sit down one day and think,
"You know what would really round me out as a
person? Turning my entire personality into a trauma
workaround."

This wasn't a rebrand.
This was an emergency setting that never shut off.

Somewhere along the way, the coping mechanisms
stopped being things I did and started being who I was.

Not metaphorically.
Functionally.

The survival settings stayed on so long they fused with
my identity like a shitty firmware update you can't
uninstall.
No rollback.
No factory reset.
Just vibes and permanent damage.

Now people don't say, "You've been through a lot."
They say, "That's just how you are."
Cool.
Love that for me.

**When Coping Stops Being a Phase and Starts Being
a Vibe**

At first, these things were situational.
Hypervigilance was a response.
Dark humor was release.
Sarcasm was armor.
Overthinking was preparation.
Dissociation was containment.
Temporary measures for a temporary hell.

Except trauma doesn't come with an expiration date.
And neither do the tools you used to survive it.
So the traits stuck.

Now I'm:
- "Intense"
- "Self-aware"
- "Funny but dark"
- "Low drama"
- "Hard to read"
- "The one who handles things"

None of these were choices.
They were adaptations that overstayed their welcome
and unpacked their bags.

Survival Skills Get Mistaken for Character Traits

This is where it gets insidious.
Hypervigilance becomes "attention to detail."
Dissociation becomes "calm under pressure."
Emotional numbness becomes "chill."
People-pleasing becomes "easygoing."
Dark humor becomes "wit."

Congratulations.

Your trauma just got promoted to personality.
And now if you stop performing it, people get weird.

People Start Expecting You to Perform It

Once it becomes your personality, people get
comfortable with it.

They expect the jokes.
They expect the insight.
They expect the self-deprecation.
They expect you to explain your own damage in a way
that reassures them.
And God forbid you don't.

If you're quiet, they worry.
If you're honest without humor, they panic.
If you're sad without packaging it, they don't know
what to do with you.

You're allowed to be messed up…
But only if you're entertaining about it.

You Don't Get to Be Soft Without Causing Concern

Try it.
Try being unsure.
Try being tired.
Try being sad without a joke attached.
Watch the room shift.

People ask if you're okay like it's an accusation.
They wait for the punchline like you owe them one.

They assume something is wrong because you're not
"being you."
Except this is you.
Just without the armor.
Apparently that's unsettling.

Self-Awareness Becomes a Trap Door

This part really fucks with you.
Once you're self-aware, people think you're done.
You can name your patterns,
so obviously you can control them.
You understand your trauma,
so clearly it shouldn't hurt anymore.
You can articulate your coping mechanisms,
so you should be finished using them.

Wrong.

Self-awareness doesn't uninstall anything.
It just means you can narrate your own collapse in real
time.

Sometimes I'm melting down while thinking,
"Wow. Look at me melting down. Fascinating."

That awareness does not stop the meltdown.
It just makes it lonelier.

Your Pain Becomes a Fun Fact

Somewhere between survival and socialization,
your pain turns into lore.
People reference it casually.
They quote you.

They reduce it to a joke you once made that made them
feel better.
"Well, you know how you are."
"That's your trauma talking."
"Classic you."

No.

Classic me was a person before this.
This is me after adapting to things that should've
broken me completely.

You Start Wondering Who You'd Be without It

This is the quiet grief nobody warns you about.
Not just grief for what happened,
but grief for who you might've been.

Who am I without:
- The constant scanning.
- The edge.
- The hyper-analysis.
- The humor that deflects instead of connects.
- The independence that came from never being
  able to rely on anyone.

I don't know.
Because trauma didn't just affect my reactions.
It shaped my interests.
My communication style.
My friendships.
My boundaries.
My tone of voice.

You can't separate the damage from the design once
it's been running this long.

You Don't Know Where Coping Ends and You Begin

This is the identity crisis nobody names.
Am I funny, or did humor keep me alive?
Am I insightful, or did hyper-analysis prevent disaster?
Am I independent, or did I learn not to need anyone
because it wasn't safe?
If you peel back the survival layers, what's underneath?

No one answers that.
Not therapists.
Not books.
Not time.
So you carry it all, even when you're exhausted from
being this person.

Trying to Change Makes Everyone Else Uncomfortable

When you soften, people don't trust it.
When you rest, they wait for collapse.
When you set boundaries, they act like you've changed.

You have.

But not in the inspirational way.

You've just gotten tired of being the version of yourself
that made everyone else comfortable.

You don't get to just be.
You get monitored.

Strength Is Only Complimented When It's Useful

People love to romanticize this.
They say:
"It made you who you are."
"You're so resilient."
"You're so strong."

What they mean is:
You adapted in a way that benefits everyone else.

Strength isn't a compliment when it's compulsory.
It's unpaid labor.

This Isn't Growth. It's Survival Fossilized

There's no reveal where the "real you" steps out from behind the damage, healed and unburdened.

There's no final form.
No reset button.
No montage.

There's just this:
If your coping mechanisms became your personality…
If people only recognize you through trauma-adapted traits…
If you don't know who you are without the armor…
You're not failing to heal.
You adapted so thoroughly that the adaptation became visible.
This is the you that survived.
Sharp.
Messy.
Tired.
Functional.

Still here.

Not because this is who you wanted to be.
But because this is who was required.

Sometimes survival doesn't end.
It settles in, learns your name,
and starts answering to it.

And you're still here anyway.
Which, honestly?
Is feral as hell.

Part IX:
Radical Reality (No Bows, No Lies)

Chapter 43
Healing Isn't a Glow-Up, It's a Maintenance Job

If you came here for the montage where I wake up cured, hydrated, and spiritually exfoliated…

Wrong fucking book.

Healing is not a makeover.
There are no before-and-after photos.
No big reveal where you suddenly trust people, enjoy mornings, and answer texts without a minor internal negotiation.

Healing is maintenance.
Unsexy.
Repetitive.
Endless.
Like owning an old, temperamental car that technically runs but will absolutely strand you on the highway at night if you stop paying attention for too long.

You don't transform.
You maintain.

Progress Is Not Forward

Let's kill the first lie:
Healing is not linear.
It's not even directional.
It's more like a drunk Roomba bouncing around your nervous system, occasionally bumping into something useful and then immediately reversing into the same wall you hit last year.

You will:
- Have good months, then crash.
- Learn a skill, and then forget it under stress.
- Feel "better," then feel exactly like you did before.
- Think you're past something, and then meet it again in a new outfit.

That's not failure.
That's the job.

Relapse Is Not a Moral Collapse

Relapse gets treated like betrayal.
Like you broke a sacred contract with healing and now everything you did before doesn't count.

People say things like:
"But you were doing so well."

Yeah.
And then life happened.

Old patterns resurface when capacity drops.
Old coping shows up when safety wobbles.
Old pain gets louder when new shit piles on.

Relapse doesn't erase progress.
It proves it existed, because you had something to fall back into.

Plateaus Are Where Healing Actually Lives

Nobody posts about plateaus.
Because they're boring.
Because they don't look like change.

Because they feel like stagnation.

Plateaus are when:
- Symptoms don't improve but also don't worsen.
- You're stable but not thriving.
- Nothing dramatic happens.

Which is infuriating in a culture obsessed with transformation.

But plateaus are maintenance mode.
They're the slow, quiet work of not falling apart.
That matters, even if it doesn't photograph well.

Regression Is Just Your Nervous System under Load

Regression doesn't mean you lost everything.
It means something overloaded you.
Stress.
Loss.
Burnout.
Illness.
Another fucking global crisis.

Your nervous system goes,
"Cool. Reverting to old settings."

Because those settings are familiar.
And familiarity feels safer than experimentation when you're exhausted.

Regression isn't a reset.
It's a fallback.

Healing Doesn't Remove the Scars

Here's the truth people keep dodging:
Healing doesn't erase what happened.
It doesn't uninstall trauma.
It doesn't cure mental illness.
It doesn't give you a clean slate.

It gives you management.

You still get triggered.
You still have bad days.
You still spiral sometimes.

The difference is subtle:
- You notice sooner.
- You recover faster.
- You punish yourself a little less brutally.

That's it.
That's the win.

The Internet Lied to You about Growth

Social media sold us a fantasy.

That healing looks like:
- Confidence
- Calm
- Clarity
- Closure

In reality, healing looks like:
- Catching yourself mid-spiral.
- Choosing the less destructive option.

- Staying when you want to disappear.
- Managing symptoms instead of conquering them.

It's not inspiring.
It's sustainable.
Which is not the same thing.

You Don't Become "Healed," You Become Experienced

Healing doesn't turn you into someone new.
It turns you into someone who knows their warning signs.

You learn:
- What drains you.
- What helps (sometimes).
- What pushes you over the edge.
- What you can't afford to ignore anymore.

That's not enlightenment.
That's familiarity.

The Goal Is Not Transformation

This might be the hardest truth in the book:
You are not becoming a different person.
You are becoming a person who knows how to live with what they carry.

Just ongoing care for a system that was injured and keeps needing attention.

Maintenance Is Not Failure

Maintenance doesn't mean you're stuck.
It means you're alive with something chronic.
People don't shame diabetics for needing insulin
forever.
But mental health?
Everyone expects a finish line.
There isn't one.
There's just upkeep.

No Big Ending…Just Continuity.

This doesn't end with triumph.
It ends with realism.

Healing didn't fix me.
It didn't save me.
It didn't turn me into someone shiny.
It taught me how to keep going without destroying
myself every time things get hard.

Some days that looks like progress.
Some days it looks like survival.
Some days it looks like regression with better language.

And that's not beautiful.
It's honest.

If healing feels boring…
If it feels repetitive…
If it feels like maintenance instead of transformation…
You're not doing it wrong.
You're doing the part no one glamorizes.

Healing isn't a glow-up.

It's showing up.
Again.
And again.
And again.

It's ongoing work of staying alive in a body and mind
that need constant care.

And that work doesn't make you impressive.
It makes you real.
And real is the only thing this book ever promised.

Chapter 44
Living With the Knowledge That This Might Always
Be Hard

There's a moment in healing nobody advertises.
It's not hopeful.
It's not empowering.
It's not the breakthrough people clap for.
It's the moment the optimism dies quietly.

Not in a blaze.
Not in a breakdown.
It just…stops showing up.

You realize you've been waiting for a moment that isn't
coming,
the one where everything finally clicks,
the weight lifts,
the symptoms fade,
and life stops feeling like a full-contact sport you didn't
train for.

And the realization lands like this:
"Oh.
This might always be hard."

Not constantly.
Not identically.

But hard enough that you notice.
Often enough that you plan around it.
Consistently enough that pretending otherwise starts to
feel insulting.

Radical Realism Is Not Pessimism

People rush to rescue you from this thought.
They say things like:
"Don't think like that."
"You can't give up hope."
"It won't always be this way."

But here's the raw truth:
Sometimes radical realism is the kindest thing you can
offer yourself.

Radical realism isn't despair.
It's inventory.

It's looking at your history, your wiring, your patterns,
your diagnoses, your nervous system, your scars, and
saying:

Okay.
This is the body and brain I have.
Not the one I wanted.
Not the one I deserved.
The one I'm living in.
That's not giving up.
That's paying attention.

The Grief No One Warned You About

There's grief for what you lost.
And then there's grief for what you never had.

The easier life.
The lighter brain.
The version of you that didn't need to work this hard
just to exist.

You grieve the fantasy of one day:
One day I'll be better.
One day I'll feel normal.
One day this won't cost so much.

Letting go of that fantasy hurts like hell.
Because hope, even false hope, was doing a lot of
emotional labor.

This grief doesn't come with casseroles or sympathy
cards.
It shows up quietly, like exhaustion.
Like bitterness you don't want to admit to.
Like watching other people stumble into ease and
wondering what you did wrong to miss that exit.

You didn't miss it.
It was never yours.

Hope Becomes Complicated

Hope used to mean:
"One day this will be over."
But what if it isn't?
What if hope gets smaller, and truer?

Hope becomes:
- Fewer catastrophic spirals.
- More neutral days.
- Knowing your patterns.
- Surviving without hating yourself every time it
  gets hard.

That hope doesn't inspire strangers.
It doesn't sell books.
It doesn't look good on a poster.

But it's real.
And real hope doesn't promise relief.
It promises endurance.

You Stop Waiting for the "After"

At some point, you realize you've been postponing
your life.

I'll live when I'm better.
I'll rest when this passes.
I'll enjoy things when I'm fixed.

And then the thought arrives, slow, heavy, unavoidable:
"What if there is no after?"
What if this is it?

That realization doesn't feel freeing.
It feels like grief with a to-do list.

But it does something important:
It stops you from bargaining with the future.
You start making decisions based on now, on what you
can actually carry, not what you wish you could.

That's not surrender.
It's clarity.

Staying Is Not Romantic

Choosing to stay doesn't feel brave.
It feels stubborn.
Petty.
Practical.

Sometimes you stay because:

- You're curious what happens next.
- You don't want to hurt people.
- You refuse to let pain have the final word.
- You're too tired to make a permanent decision.

That's not inspirational.
It's honest.

You don't stay because you believe everything will be okay.

You stay because leaving isn't the answer either.

You're allowed to Hate That This Is Hard

Acceptance doesn't mean liking it.
You can accept reality and still be furious about it.
You can say:
"This is my life,"
and also say,
"This is unfair."

Both can exist.

Acceptance isn't peace.
It's refusing to lie to yourself just to make other people more comfortable.

Some Days, Staying Is the Only Goal

There are days when:
Joy isn't available.
Growth isn't available.
Healing isn't available.

Staying is.

Staying alive.
Staying present.
Staying long enough for the day to end.

That's not failure.
That's the work.

This Is Not Resignation

This is not about surrendering to misery.
It's about dropping the fantasy that one day you'll wake
up cured and everything will make sense.

It's about building a life that fits around the hard parts
instead of waiting for them to disappear.

That's not giving up.
That's adaptation.

The Choices You Make Repeatedly

There is no final acceptance.
No moment where you're at peace with the fact that this
might always be hard.

There's just a decision you make again and again:
"I'll stay today."
Not forever.
Not heroically.
Today.

If you're living with the knowledge that this might
always be hard…

If you're grieving the life you wanted while still
showing up for the one you have…
If staying feels less like hope and more like stubborn
endurance…
You're not weak.
You're not broken.
You're not failing to heal.
You're being honest about reality.

And choosing to stay anyway, without guarantees,
without promises, without a happy ending…
Is not beautiful.
It's not brave.
It's just real.

And sometimes, real is the strongest thing there is.

Just the quiet, repeated choice to stay, even knowing it
might never get easy.

That choice is the story.

Chapter 45
No Happy Ending, Just a Tomorrow

There isn't a happy ending.

Not the kind people want.
Not the kind that wraps everything up, teaches a lesson,
hands you closure like a gift receipt, and fades out on a
satisfied sigh.

There's just…tomorrow.
And that's honestly rude.

If you came here looking for the part where I tell you it
was all worth it,
where the pain finds meaning,
where suffering becomes wisdom,
where I ride off into the emotionally regulated sunset…
This is not that book.

There is no happy ending here.
There is just tomorrow.

Hope Is Not the Hero of This Story

Hope gets way too much credit.
Hope is fragile.
Hope is flaky.
Hope disappears the second things get hard.

If I waited for hope, I would not be here.

Hope requires belief.
Belief requires safety.
Safety was not consistently available.
So I didn't build my survival on hope.

I built it on something smaller.
Meaner.
More reliable.

Momentum.
Spite.
Routine.
The sheer refusal to let a bad moment be the final edit.

Hope-as-a-platitude can fuck all the way off.

I don't need "It gets better."
I don't need "Everything happens for a reason."
I don't need "You're stronger than you think."
I need honesty.

Tomorrow Is Not a Promise. It's a Placeholder.

Tomorrow doesn't mean things will improve.
Tomorrow doesn't guarantee relief, insight, or growth.
Tomorrow just means:
This day ends.
That's it.

No emotional breakthrough.
No lesson learned.
No redemption montage.
Just the quiet, brutal fact that time keeps moving
whether you're ready or not.

And sometimes that's the only mercy on offer.

Tomorrow isn't hope.
Tomorrow is logistics.
Wake up.
Drink water.

Avoid the abyss until noon.
Repeat.

I Didn't Keep Going Because Life Was Good

Let's be clear.
I didn't keep going because:
- I found purpose.
- I healed completely.
- I discovered joy.
- I unlocked the secret of happiness.

I kept going because stopping felt final.
And I wasn't ready for final.

That's not inspirational.
That's survival math.

Some days are tolerable.
Some days are not.

Some days are a weird, exhausting mix of both that
leaves you tired in a way sleep doesn't touch.

Tomorrow isn't a gift.
It's a coin flip.

Choosing Tomorrow Is Not Optimism

Choosing tomorrow doesn't mean you believe things
will get better.
It means you're willing to tolerate uncertainty.

It means you're saying:
"I don't know what comes next, and I'll stay anyway."

That's not hope.
That's endurance with a pulse.

People think survival is about believing in a future.
Sometimes it's just refusing to end the story on a bad
chapter.

Some Days, Tomorrow Is All You Can Manage

There are days when:
- You don't feel grateful.
- You don't feel strong.
- You don't feel resilient.
- You don't feel anything except tired.

On those days, tomorrow is enough.

Not because it's exciting.
Because it's possible.

You don't choose forever.
You choose the next hour.
The next task.
The next breath that doesn't require a philosophy.

It sounds like:
"I'll deal with this later."
"I'll eat something and see how I feel."
"I'll make it to bedtime."
"I'll reassess in the morning."

Small.
Unimpressive.
Deeply human.

Living without a Happy Ending Is Still Living

We are obsessed with closure.
Redemptions.
Meaningful suffering.
Lessons neatly learned.

Real life doesn't do that.
Sometimes pain doesn't resolve.
Sometimes answers never come.
Sometimes you don't get to feel okay about what
happened.

And you still wake up the next day.

Not healed.
Not inspired.
Just here.

That counts, even if no one claps.

This Is Not a Call to Be Brave

I'm not going to tell you you're brave for staying.

Sometimes staying doesn't feel brave.

It feels annoying.
Petty.
Exhausting.
Automatic.

Like breathing when you're not sure why you're still
bothering.

That still counts.

Anger is energy.
Spite is fuel.
Routine is scaffolding.
Dark humor is duct tape.
Use whatever works.

You Don't Need to Make Meaning Out of This

You don't owe anyone a lesson.
You don't owe the pain a purpose.
You don't owe survival a moral.
You don't need to justify why you stayed.

Staying is not a speech.
It's an action.

Repeated.

Often reluctantly.

Tomorrow Doesn't Ask Much of You

Tomorrow doesn't require motivation.
It doesn't require growth.
It doesn't require positivity.

It just asks:
"Are you still here?"

And sometimes the honest answer is:
"Reluctantly."

That's still an answer.

No Ending…Just Continuation.

This book doesn't end with healing.
It ends with continuity.

With an open calendar and a nervous system that's
learned to negotiate instead of surrender.

You didn't get a happy ending.
You got another day.
And another.
And another.

Not because life finally made sense,
but because you kept choosing not today over the
illusion of finality.

That's not beautiful.
It's not poetic.
It's effective.

No answers.
No bullshit.
No happy ending.
Just tomorrow.

And for now?

That's the whole fucking point.